God Who?

Sarah Elizabeth Coleman

God Who?

Knowing the God You Believe In

REVIEW AND HERALD® PUBLISHING ASSOCIATION
HAGERSTOWN, MD 21740

The author assumes full responsibility for the accuracy of all facts and quotations as cited in this book.

This book was
Edited by Jeannette R. Johnson
Copyedited by Jocelyn Fay and James Cavil
Designed by Willie Duke
Electronic makeup by Shirley M. Bolivar
Typeset: 11/14 Garamond Light

PRINTED IN U.S.A.

03 02 01 00 99 5 4 3 2 1

R&H Cataloging Service
Coleman, Sarah Elizabeth, 1977-
God who?

1. God I. Title

231

ISBN 0-8280-1354-3

This book is dedicated to
Chris, Charley, Aaron, Renee, Alex, Caroline,
and all those who care enough to ask;

and

to Angie,
who endures my searching so patiently.

Thank you.

Contents

Introduction

God Who?

"A-a-a-a-my! Your taco's ready!" A food service worker yells from behind the counter.

A ponytailed girl stands to retrieve her order. The student activity center (SAC) pulses with late-night college life. Ryan, in contrast to the chaos around him, hasn't spoken for the past five minutes. He bulldozes a cold wedge of pizza around his plate and pokes it with a plastic fork, waiting for my response.

What should I say? I pick at my own greasy slice of pizza absentmindedly. Ryan has spent the past half hour pouring out his problems to me. I know he's waiting for my usual burst of encouragement. But tonight, for some inexplicable reason, I'm tongue-tied.

Behind us a cash register drawer slams shut.

Why can't I say it? *Everything will be just fine . . .* The thought forms in my mind, but the words won't escape. *God will take care of everything—won't He?*

Ryan begins methodically wadding and unwadding his napkin. As I stare at the hopeless expression on his face, I slowly realize my own problem. *I've been doling out ready-made encouragement like free stop-smoking pamphlets. I don't even know what I've been saying!*

"Ryan, do you believe in God?"

He glances up, his napkin forgotten. "Uh, yeah." He fumbles. "Of course I do. I mean, I believe in *something* . . ." His voice trails off, and he runs a hand through his dark brown hair.

"What?" I ask eagerly. "Tell me what you believe in. I want to know." Suddenly I realize that I need to answer the question as much as Ryan does.

We spend the rest of our conversation describing a faith we don't understand. But when I walk back to my dorm, I still haven't reached any conclusions. Alone on the dimly lit sidewalk, I feel very far from the God I should know already.

Who are You, God?

I shiver in the sharp December air. How can I claim to be a Christian when I don't know Christ?

But, I think as I pull open the heavy dorm door, *I'll know Him soon.* During our conversation in the SAC I resolved to find God for myself. And I know my integrity will never let me give up.

"Who is God?" "Who says He exists?" "How do you know?" "Can you prove it?" In a yearlong chain of late-night conversations, early-morning jogs, and solitary silences, I've been searching for answers to a growing mountain of questions. As I search, I discover more and more people who ask the same questions. They too face silent Bibles and blank stares. They feel hypocritical attending a church they don't understand and praying to a God they don't know. They too want to know God on more than a first-name basis.

God *who?* is my attempt to know Him better—and share Him with those who ask the same question. During that conversation in the SAC I asked "God *who?*" in the same way that a person asks "Jessica *who?*" when meeting a new acquaintance. I was (and am) honestly curious about God's countless "last names." And the ideas in this book only begin the list of possibilities.

Please read on. And read with an open heart. I encourage you to argue with anything you disagree with. Write in the margins. Tell your own story. Go ahead and call me, if you want. Do whatever it takes to help you formulate your own list of "last names" for God—a list that only you can understand completely, a list you can rely on when someone asks you "God *who?*" in the future.

May God of the Searching bless you as you continue.

—Sarah

Reference Points:

"My soul yearns, even faints, for the courts of the Lord; my heart and my flesh cry out for the living God" (Psalm 84:2).

"Jesus answered, 'I am the way and the truth and the life. No one comes to the Father except through me'" (John 14:6).

"Hear my cry, O God; listen to my prayer. From the ends of the earth I call to you, I call as my heart grows faint; lead me to the rock that is higher than I" (Psalm 61:1, 2).

"You will seek me and find me when you seek me with all your heart" (Jeremiah 29:13).

"As the deer pants for streams of water, so my soul pants for you, O God. My soul thirsts for God, for the living God. When can I go and meet with God? My tears have been my food day and night, while men say to me all day long, 'Where is your God?' . . . Why are you downcast, O my soul? Why so disturbed within me? Put your hope in God, for I will yet praise him, my Savior and my God" (Psalm 42:1-5).

Chapter One

God *the Real*

I scuff along the highway's edge, kicking at loose chunks of blacktop and rocks. "I don't know what to do!" I storm, wondering how Braden can possibly understand. "I've known about God for years. People have quoted Bible verses to me all my life. I grew up on Sabbath school quarterlies and Ellen White devotionals. I'm nothing more than a product of my Christian environment!"

"Is that so terrible?" Braden asks innocently.

"For me, yes." I take a deep breath and continue. "Braden, I feel brainwashed into believing in God."

Braden stops walking. "But I thought you had a strong relationship with God!"

"I do." I kick angrily at a clump of grass. "I mean, I *did.* But what if that relationship is just someone else's experience wrapped up and labeled with my name?"

Braden spreads his hands, palms up. "I can't answer that question."

"I know. I don't want you to answer it. But I *do* want a faith of my own." I glare up at the unresponsive sky. "I want to know God for myself. *Without* any help from *Our Little Friend."* I'm silent for a while, lost in the thoughts I can't explain even to my closest friends.

"I understand what you want." Braden plucks a tall flag of cheat grass from the roadside and places it firmly between his teeth. "But how will you get it?" He chews the stem distractedly.

"I don't know. But I don't want anything from the past to affect my decision, so I'm going to throw it all out!"

Braden's eyebrows raise. "How?"

"I'm going to pretend that there is no God, and then look for evidence to prove He exists. That way I won't have any preconceived ideas to weight my decision. Simple, huh?" I hold my breath. Somehow Braden's opinion seems very important to the success of my plan.

He clears his throat. "Are you sure that's a good idea?"

"Hey!" I punch him in the arm. "You sound skeptical! What's wrong?"

"Well, I don't know," he admits. "But I think you're using some faulty logic."

"OK, tell me what you think." I clamp my mouth shut and wait for his honest opinion.

"Well," Braden stares intently at his blade of grass as though its stalk can help him speak. To our right, the wind tosses a greening wheat field into a frenzy of waves.

"Am *I* real?" He finally speaks into our silence.

"Of course!" I laugh. "That's a silly question."

"Exactly. But can you *prove* that I'm real?"

I giggle. "Braden, I know you. I talk with you. Of course you're real!"

He holds up a silencing hand. "If you denied my existence, would I still be real?"

"Y-e-e-e-s." I bite my lower lip and look away.

"If you wanted to prove my existence, wouldn't it be easier to talk to me in person?" He grins. "What can you lose? If I wasn't real, you'd find out soon enough. But if I am real, you'll have a head start on everyone else who's searching."

I rub my forehead. "This applies to God, doesn't it?" I ask wearily. "You think the same philosophy works with Him, right?"

Braden nods and studies my face. His forgotten piece of grass drops to the highway, as useless as my once-perfect plan for action.

"Well, I don't know what to say. I'll have to think about it for a while."

Good old Braden. In a few minutes' time he effectively showed me what I couldn't see for myself.

Yes, I decide. *Yes, I'm tired of being told what to believe. I wish I could erase my past and get a fresh start at discovering God. I feel brainwashed with Jesus-loves-me songs and Uncle Arthur stories.* I sigh and stare at the far-off horizon. *But that doesn't mean I should deny that He exists in order to find Him again.*

Braden and I spend the rest of our walk chatting about other subjects. Ambling down the crumbling blacktop, we reminisce about our academy days. But my mind reserves a huge corner strictly for analyzing Braden's proposal.

After we finally say goodbye, I walk back to my dorm in silence. Occasionally I glance up at the cloud-rimmed sky. As I walk, I'm slowly rephrasing my question for God. *God, You're not real. Can You prove me wrong?* becomes *God, are You real? I'm willing to listen.*

God *who*? God the Real. So real that despite my own doubts and questions He retains His identity. God the Real, whose reality I'm still trying to comprehend. God the Real, who loves to show Himself to those who wonder. Whose reality exists in the lives of those like Braden who know Him well.

Reference Points:

"We have put our hope in the living God, who is the Savior of all men, and especially of those who believe" (1 Timothy 4:10).

"If you confess with your mouth, 'Jesus is Lord,' and believe in your heart that God raised him from the dead, you will be saved. For it is with your heart that you believe and are justified, and it is with your mouth that you confess and are saved" (Romans 10:9, 10).

"Without faith it is impossible to please God, because anyone who comes to him must believe that he exists and that he rewards those who earnestly seek him" (Hebrews 11:6).

Chapter Two

God *the Relevant*

Dear God,

It has been a very long time since I spoke to You. So to lessen the shock of my sudden reappearance, I'm writing to You instead. (I'm not sure how to address the envelope, but that's a trivial detail.)

You must wonder how I've been lately, and to tell the truth . . .

Dear God,

It has been a very long time since You spoke to me. In fact, I don't remember ever hearing Your voice directly. What does it sound like? Are You a baritone? a bass? Somehow I can't picture You as a tenor. What does Divinity say when He wants to contact humanity? "Heaven to Earth, this is God. Put Me through to Room 268"?

I would have answered Your call. But I don't think You tried. I would have heard You; I have great ears. Besides, it's highly unlikely that I would miss such an important . . .

Dear God,

Would You like to communicate? Why don't You

share a little first? Like strength, maybe. Or maybe some faith. Of course, I could always use a new car, but today I'm asking for something a little more lasting, that would make me feel more secure about . . .

Dear God,

I know, I know. You probably hate unfinished letters. But hey, if You're half the God You claim to be, You can complete my sentences anyway. Besides, most of the stuff I want to write could be used against me in court. I'm trying to keep my record as spotless as possible. That way when I decide to do something really terrible, the police will think it was just a mistake.

God, there's something I've been meaning to ask You. I can't concentrate long enough to beat around the bush when I pray. I end up thinking about Spanish or jogging or guys. I hope I still have Your full attention after all those practice letters.

You've probably recovered from Your initial surprise that yes, I am writing to You again. You've probably moved on to more interesting letters. Like the kind little kids write that somebody collects in sweet little books. They're so cute. The letters, I mean. I wonder if You hang them on Your refrigerator. (I wonder if You even have a refrigerator?)

So, as I was saying, why don't I finish this letter when I know what to say?

Dear God,

OK, I'll get it out in the open! The least I can do is erase it when I'm done. Or burn it. Or . . .

Sorry.

God, who says You're relevant?

(Oops, I'm writing with pen. Pretend You didn't see that. I can't think of anything else to . . .)

Dear God,

This is fun. Writing to You makes You seem like an imaginary friend, and that's more real than You've ever seemed before.

Did You get my last letter? It was a compilation of several witty sentence fragments. I threw it in the trash can behind my bedroom door if You want to read it. Of course, if You're too busy answering the 1-800 line, I understand . . .

God,

I decided to drop the "dear." It's hypocritical anyway. If You reply, I might start writing "dear" again. Tempting, isn't it? I'll bet You can hardly restrain Yourself from grabbing the nearest pen and scribbling something across the night sky.

What am I saying? It's 11:00 in the morning!

God,

That's kind of a pretentious title, don't You think? Why not try something a little more realistic, like Man Made of Clouds or The Great Invisible Security Blanket or I Only Speak to Parents, Teachers, and Pastors?

God.

I mean, that's so final. It's so self-assured. It's so *short!*

If You really want to impress humanity, You should at least sign Your name "God, Esq." or "God, Ph.D." or something. This whole one-syllable "God" business makes it sound as though You think You're already perfect enough.

You know, that's another thing I've been wondering. And it's a little safer to talk about than relevance. (Oops. You didn't see that either.)

Do You ever mess up? I mean, just something little? Say, in the morning when You're brushing Your teeth? Do You ever accidentally spit a little toothpaste foam onto the mirror? Or maybe it dribbles down Your chin before You can catch it? Don't You get tired of being so clean all the time? I would. That's why I never clean my room unless Mom's coming to . . .

God,

Another unfinished epistle. I wonder if anybody else does this. Maybe Your disciples. They probably thought You might change Your mind and come back to live in Jerusalem after all. And when You did, they'd have a big stack of letters to catch You up on all the latest gossip.

All right, all right. It's been several weeks now. I'll ask You again, since You obviously didn't get my hint and read that letter I left in my trash can.

Kind of strange. Delivering letters to God in a trash can.

Right. Here we go.

God, who says You're relevant?

I mean, really. If You're so powerful, why can't You take a few milliseconds from Your busy schedule to remind us here on the Failed Experiment Planet that You still exist? You're all we have, You know. Other planets can just sit and bask in their perfection and never have to clean toothpaste off their mirrors, but we're pretty much doomed to self-destruct any day now.

I know the Bible claims that You died for us. And I think that it's great to have such a pretty story written down in such an important book. But I want to hear it from the horse's mouth, so to speak.

Did You really die for *us*? Me included? And if You did, why can't I see more evidence of You now? Bible classes and sermons do not count. I want cold, hard . . .

God,

Sorry. I know that was an important thought and all, but someone called. It was a boy, actually. And I figure since You don't take time for me, why should I worry about an unfinished sentence here and there?

We talked for a long time, God, this boy and I. We have the same questions about certain things. You, for example. So we're ganging up on You. We want to know that You still exist. That You are [drumroll, please] relevant.

I feel as though I've been praying to the Easter Bunny all my life. I'd like to see a little more than some old painted eggs. Why not a miracle, God? An all-out, rootin'-tootin' miracle that . . .

God,

He called again. It was nice. Are You jealous?

Sorry. We talked about it, and I've decided not to be so cynical with You. I mean, what if You actually *are* relevant? What if You are more than an old man with Alzheimer's who makes perfect wood carvings all day and takes out His hearing aid to avoid interruptions? What if You're young—drinking from the fountain of youth or something? Oh, yeah—You probably created the fountain of youth.

At any rate, I'm here to tell You that I will take You seriously from now on. Not that You've given me any reason to take You seriously lately, but I really do want to hear from You.

Really.

I won't hold You to the rootin'-tootin' miracle bit, all right? But it *was* pretty witty. At this point, I'll accept whatever You give me. I'll try to stay open to the fact that You might be a tenor. Or that You might not speak at all when You want my attention.

I'll even stop kidding You about the toothpaste.

See? I'm prepared to listen. Or look. Or whatever You want me to do. I'll do it, I promise. Just talk to me! I can't explain why, but it's very important to my future happiness that I know if You're relevant. I'll even *wait* for an answer, if You want me to. Now that's a big step in the right . . .

Dear God,

He called again. Just as I was sitting there smiling because I knew I'd finally given You a chance to speak. Just then, he called.

And then, well, You know what happened. We went for a drive to the mountains to find a Christmas tree. And then the truck started spinning. And then it rolled into a snowbank. And then I don't remember. And then it was really dark and he was saying, "Are you all right? Are you all right?"

And then I said, "Yes, I think."

And then he said, "Thank God."

Just like that.

We climbed out of the truck and stood in the snow, and I shivered. Next thing I knew, a state trooper drove by, and we sat in his car while Mr. Tow Truck drove up to pull the truck out.

It was all so simple.

The insurance man said the truck's frame was so twisted that we were lucky to be alive. A window shattered in my face, and I didn't get cut. God, he wasn't even wearing his seat belt! How do You do that?

I'll have to admit I'm impressed.

I still don't know if You're a tenor or not. I guess it isn't that important. I do know that You talked to me, though. Talked to *us*.

I'm sure it was fun, planning that perfect accident so we'd end up saying "Thank God." In a way, I guess, it was kind of fun to be in it, too. Thank You, God.

Hey, I actually finished a letter! Save it for Your scrapbook.

I know You may not speak so loudly all the time. That's OK. I know the next time I ask You for a sign, You may not send one. That's OK too. And I know that when I tell this story to other people, it may not even affect them. I can cope.

Because now I know. Now I know that no matter how silent You seem, You will pull through when I need it the most. I know You speak in a million voices, and I must listen with as many ears. I know, after an eternity of writing letters to the Easter Bunny god, that You are much, much more than that. You are God, my God, the one who is relevant to me—and I'm beginning to love You.

That's the best conversation-starter I've thought of in a long time. I wonder what You would do if I actually *spoke* to You . . .

Reference Points:

"Oh, the depth of the riches of the wisdom and knowledge of God! How unsearchable his judgments, and his paths beyond tracing out! 'Who has known the mind of the Lord? Or who has been his counselor?' 'Who has ever given to God, that God should repay him?' For from him and through him and to him are all things. To

him be the glory forever! Amen" (Romans 11:33-36).

"The Lord said, 'Go out and stand on the mountain in the presence of the Lord, for the Lord is about to pass by.' Then a great and powerful wind tore the mountains apart and shattered the rocks before the Lord, but the Lord was not in the wind. After the wind there was an earthquake, but the Lord was not in the earthquake. After the earthquake came a fire, but the Lord was not in the fire. And after the fire came a gentle whisper. When Elijah heard it, he pulled his cloak over his face and went out and stood at the mouth of the cave. Then a voice said to him, 'What are you doing here, Elijah?'" (1 Kings 19:11-13).

"Ascribe to the Lord the glory due his name; worship the Lord in the splendor of his holiness. The voice of the Lord is over the waters; the God of glory thunders, the Lord thunders over the mighty waters. The voice of the Lord is powerful; the voice of the Lord is majestic. The voice of the Lord breaks the cedars; the Lord breaks in pieces the cedars of Lebanon. He makes Lebanon skip like a calf, Sirion like a young wild ox. The voice of the Lord strikes with flashes of lightning. The voice of the Lord shakes the desert; the Lord shakes the Desert of Kadesh. The voice of the Lord twists the oaks and strips the forests bare. And in his temple all cry, 'Glory!'" (Psalm 29:2-9).

Chapter Three

God *Who Fulfills*

Pull, crackle, step. Pull, crackle, step. Pull, crackle—

Alex and I follow each other around a huge circle of leaves. Ahead of me, he pulls them to the middle, heaps them up, and moves forward again. My actions mirror his, and the two of us create a rustling rhythm.

Pull, crackle, step. Pull, crackle, step . . .

My thoughts chase each other in much the same pattern. *I . . . love . . . fall. I . . . love . . . fall.* All around us leaves sift to the ground like red and brown confetti. Cool enough to invite a sweatshirt, the air reddens our cheeks and noses. And despite the nearness of winter, the sky remains a vibrant blue. *It's good to be alive,* I decide, smiling at Alex's flanneled back.

Suddenly the flannel turns, and I see a row of buttons instead. "Sarah, do you think anyone can live a fulfilling life without God?" Alex asks, not breaking his *pull-crackle-step* rhythm.

Faced with his back once again, my smile falters and falls. *Why did you have to bring God into the picture?* I mentally grumble. *I'd almost forgotten about the whole mess!* My green rake clutches at the leaves and digs furrows in the rumpled grass. "What do *you* think?" I finally shoot back.

"I asked you first."

I stab at the air with my rake. I knew he'd say that. For nearly a year I've come to Alex with my doubts about God. But lately I've gotten so tired of asking questions that I no longer voice them to my friends. Now, it seems, Alex has decided to remind me of my search.

Pull, crackle, step. I jerk free of our rhythm and stalk toward a nearby oak tree to rake alone. "Give me a few minutes, OK?"

"Sure."

I rake the scattered leaves into a pile near the trunk. *Can anyone live a fulfilling life without God?* The question, like so many others I've asked in the past year, just won't leave my mind.

Pull, crackle, step. Behind me, Alex's rhythm continues. My mind flies as fast as the leaves I rake. Fifteen minutes wing by.

"OK, I'm ready to talk," I finally call to Alex's busy-looking profile.

He grins, shoulders his rake, and saunters toward me. "Go for it."

"Well, it's kind of complicated," I begin.

"That's all right."

I take a deep breath. "I'm a pretty happy person, right?"

"Uh, usually."

I punch his arm. "Yes, I am. And I've stayed happy through all these questions, even though I haven't been close to God."

Alex nods, his expression suddenly serious.

"There are probably millions of people out there just like me," I continue. "They live their lives about like mine—somewhere between seeking and finding God. And they're pretty happy." I think about my non-Christian friends. "In fact, most of them are good people. They give money to charity organizations, they feed their animals, they recycle soda cans. They probably like their lives."

"Are you sure?" Alex has to ask.

I kick at a tree root. "Well, I haven't *asked* them, but they seem to be happy." I pause and smile at Alex's downcast face. "Don't worry, I'm not finished. To find true fulfillment people need to devote their lives to something they love—something that will love them back. Right?"

"Yeah." Alex twirls his rake handle like a baton. "Something that will give them hope."

"Exactly." I nod. "Well, while I was raking, I thought of all the things that my friends turn to for fulfillment: money, friends, children, music, or a job."

"Or relationships."

"Yeah. And I thought, *Those things can make you happy, but they can't give true fulfillment. Money can't love you back. Friends can't give you hope. Children turn on you; love goes sour; and music and work are pretty impersonal, in the long run.*"

"So what does that mean?" Alex's blue eyes watch me intently.

I stare at the grass. "I guess it means that nothing on this earth will provide true fulfillment."

"So?" Alex prods.

"So the only thing left is something supernatural."

"God!" The smile spreads across his face like sunlight on a lake.

"Yes, but that doesn't mean I understand Him." I finally meet his eyes, round like scraps of the clear sky above us. "All I'm saying is that I don't think anything on earth could be completely fulfilling. And that leaves me and every other person with a choice: Do we want to be mostly happy all our lives, or do we want to search for the God who claims to offer more? Either way, it's a pretty big risk." I pick up my rake and take a step backward.

Alex's face is a picture of happiness. "You'll take that risk," he prophesies joyfully. "I know you will."

"Maybe."

I want to wipe the smile off his face. *How do you know what I'll do? How do you know I won't be content to stay "mostly happy" for the rest of my life? You haven't won any battles, Alex. Don't celebrate too soon.*

But as his *pull, crackle, step* continues behind me, I have to admit that I feel better than I have in months. I've finally found an answer to one of my questions. And I know, as I rake across the front campus lawn on that mostly happy afternoon, that I'm willing to take any risk to find ultimate happiness, the kind of happiness that only a God who fulfills can provide.

Reference Points:

"The Lord will guide you always; he will satisfy your needs in a sun-

scorched land and will strengthen your frame. You will be like a well-watered garden, like a spring whose waters never fail" (Isaiah 58:11).

"You have made known to me the path of life; you will fill me with joy in your presence, with eternal pleasures at your right hand" (Psalm 16:11).

"Delight yourself in the Lord and he will give you the desires of your heart. Commit your way to the Lord; trust in him and he will do this" (Psalm 37:4, 5).

"What good is it for a man to gain the whole world, yet forfeit his soul? Or what can a man give in exchange for his soul?" (Mark 8:36, 37).

Chapter Four

God *I Need*

I'm a pretty happy person . . . My recent words echo in my mind as I stare through bloodshot eyes at my pulsating computer screen. *I'm a pretty happy . . .*

"I can't stand it!" I slam my literature textbook shut and stalk from the room. At 2:00 in the morning my attention span has dwindled to five-minute bursts of rational thought. Too much stress bombards my mind. Too many questions beg for answers. And too many deadlines loom in my future. The combination of family, friends, school, and work threatens to send me to an asylum if I don't calm down. Soon.

As I pace the blue halls of my dorm, my own words still haunt me. *I'm a pretty happy person . . . without God.* Had I told the truth?

I pause in a muddy stairwell to gather my wits. The chilly air from an open window cools my burning forehead, and I lean against its smudged pane in relief. As I stare across the night-darkened campus, my mind wanders back to another day of work for Grounds . . .

"Come get this pile!" I wave at Angie, who sits atop a tractor like a tiny bird in a loud green tree.

She grins and maneuvers the vehicle toward me. A wide green trailer bumps along behind her, sporting a mouthful of teeth painted across its back end. I smile at the mouth from whose jaws extend a long hose that hungrily inhales our leaf piles.

"Stop!" I yell.

Angie halts the monster. She jumps from her perch, and we both start shoveling a pile of leaves toward the hose. As I paw the damp leaves, I gaze around our front campus lawn. *Beautiful!* Autumn has not yet stripped the trees of all their color. Reds, yellows, and earthy oranges tickle my eyes. Sunlight filters through the canopy and creates little dots of brightness all along the grass. I feel invincible.

"Angie!" I shout, suddenly inspired. "Let me drive this thing to the next pile!"

"Are you sure?" Angie, well aware of my mechanical shortcomings, makes a face at me. "I don't think that's a good idea."

But the beauty of the day has bewitched me. "Sure it is! Just tell me what to do!" I leap to the seat of the tractor and feel its great iron heart pulsing beneath me.

"Push that lever forward," Angie yells doubtfully. "And then you can—"

Her next words disappear in the roar of the engine. *The lever!* I grab it and push it as far forward as it will go.

"Wait!" Angie's cry comes too late. Moving faster than any tractor I've ever seen, the awakened beast plows across the lawn. I clamp my arms around the steering wheel and twist it with all the force in my body. Close-set trees flash by like graphics on a computer game. Ahead of me loom a tight-packed line of trees and a steep downward slope. *I can't stop!* I yank on switches and knobs across the huge panel, but nothing slows my speed. Visions of mangled metal and crushed people flash through my mind. The tractor speeds on, oblivious to my impending death.

"Pull down! Pull down! *Pull down!"* Angie's voice filters into my blurring consciousness.

I fumble for the lever and pull with all my might. The snarling tractor purrs once again, and the engine sputters to silence. The only sound left is Angie's loud huffing beside me as we turn to survey the aftermath of my adventure. Deep tire tracks trace uprooted strips of grass where I spun out and continue in a series of impossible curves.

"Why don't you drive for a while?" I slide weakly from the seat. "You can give me lessons later, all right?"

Angie nods. "Now, *that's* a good idea." Her brown freckles on her nose stand out in sharp contrast to her pale skin.

I smile—and suddenly I'm back in my dorm again, my forehead pressed against a steamed-up window. *I'm glad to be alive,* I realize with a start. *I wouldn't miss this rain-soaked evening for anything in the world!* I shiver and turn from the window. *But I don't think I'll solo on a tractor anytime soon! I've learned my lesson—for now.*

I'll never be a mechanical genius. I've nearly killed myself on almost every kind of vehicle I've driven. After countless close calls, however, I have finally learned my limitations. I can't step onto anything and instantly understand how it works. No matter how much college education I receive, I'll always need some help.

I'm not *a pretty happy person without God.*

The realization hits me with the same chill as the windowpane that cooled my forehead. *And I'm not a nice person without God, either. I'm not loving. I'm not giving. I'm not selfless.* An entire list of shortcomings bombards my mind. I remember long-held grudges, late-night fights, unspoken competitions, and thoughtless insults. The road to perfection seems as long as the eternal corridor reflected in the mirror at the end of my hall. *No matter how hard I try, I'll always need some help.*

Inwardly I groan and slide from the tractor seat of self-assurance that I've occupied for so long. I know I'll never take full credit for my good points again. *I can't do this alone,* I admit, surveying the obstacle course my life has become. *I'm going to cause some serious damage if I keep driving.*

My next thoughts are fuzzy and incredibly hard to articulate, but I continue. *Why don't You drive for a while?* I invite my silent Witness. *I may be mostly happy on my own, but I realize now that I desperately need You to complete my character. You can give me lessons.*

Somewhere, I know the God I need is smiling.

Reference Points:

"So, if you think you are standing firm, be careful that you don't fall" (1 Corinthians 10:12).

"He will respond to the prayer of the destitute; he will not despise their plea" (Psalm 102:17).

"'Lord, if it's you,' Peter replied, 'tell me to come to you on the water.' 'Come,' he said. Then Peter got down out of the boat, walked on the water and came toward Jesus. But when he saw the wind, he was afraid and, beginning to sink, cried out, 'Lord, save me!'" (Matthew 14:28, 29).

"When he saw the crowds, he had compassion on them, because they were harassed and helpless, like sheep without a shepherd" (Matthew 9:36).

"The eternal God is your refuge, and underneath are the everlasting arms" (Deuteronomy 33:27).

"If we claim to be without sin, we deceive ourselves and the truth is not in us" (1 John 1:8).

Chapter Five

God the Big

"We have a story for you," Grandma begins one lazy summer evening.

Charley and I grin. "About what?"

"A rattlesnake." Grandpa shifts his weight to the other work-booted foot and adjusts his ever-present toothpick to a perfect angle.

I shudder, well aware of the healthy reptile population on our land.

"Grandpa and I were sitting on the porch one day," Grandma begins, "and we were almost asleep."

I picture the two of them leaning against each other, eyes half closed, on their old blue plastic swing.

Grandma continues. "Just as I dozed off, Grandpa tapped my arm. I opened my eyes and watched as a huge rattler slithered across the lawn, straight toward us!"

"No!" Charley bursts out.

"Yes," Grandpa picks up the story. "He was a big one."

Grandma makes a circle with her hands that's as big as my upper arm. "And he didn't make any noise. If we hadn't seen him, I think he would have joined us on the porch!"

The skin on my back tingles as I imagine a huge silent snake slithering onto our own front porch. "Of course you killed him—didn't you?"

They nod solemnly, and I let out my breath in

relief. "Good!" I live in constant fear of meeting a rattlesnake face-to-fang. In the morning, when I jog up our gravel road, I watch the sagebrush for suspicious-looking shapes. When I ride my bike cross-country, every crackling pile of leaves sounds like the rattle of an angry snake. And despite all my bravado, I still jump at strange noises in the grass. Thankfully, I've never had to wrestle one single-handedly. In fact, the closest I've come to actually touching a rattlesnake is through Grandpa's impressive collection of rattles. It sits in a dusty jar on the entryway counter. Periodically he pulls out the collection and tells me the stories behind each rattle.

"This one," he explains, pulling out a yellowed specimen and placing it in my quivering hands, "came from a three-foot monster. Boy, was he angry! He came a-slitherin' out of that den prepared to bite the first thing he laid eyes on. Luckily, that thing was my .22 rifle."

I shudder.

"And this one," Grandpa continues, holding up a tiny button of a rattle, "came from a baby rattler who was sunning himself right beside the fence. The fence that I'd just jumped over, mind you." He looks at me to judge my reaction. "Baby rattlers have the strongest venom."

I nod, properly awed, and respectfully return the first rattle to the jar.

Can you imagine the insult I'd give Grandpa if I refused to believe him? *Can you prove those rattles came from snakes? I think you just bought them at a cheap Halloween shop. In fact, I don't even think rattlers are dangerous at all. Prove it!*

Grandpa would be irate. Of course rattlesnakes are dangerous! Of course they're big! Just because I haven't seen one wave its talking tail at me doesn't mean a thing. Even if I see only a small piece of the picture and hear the stories of those who know, I should have enough faith to believe this creature exists.

I can't see the full picture of God, either. I know Him through what I see on my own—the Bible, miracles, nature, and prayer—and through the stories of those who know Him. But I've never watched Him answer a thousand prayers at once. I've never seen Him set the sun to moving. I haven't seen Him plan the future. I must accept that, along with His title, God carries an identity bigger than anything I can comprehend.

God *who*? God the Big, the one who fashioned my life out of thin air; who blows the wind across fields of wheat in chase-tag patterns; who consistently sends me enough oxygen and energy to live another day; who waits in a heaven I've never seen to welcome me into an equally big eternity with Him.

Reference Points:

"That day when evening came, he said to his disciples, 'Let us go over to the other side.' Leaving the crowd behind, they took him along, just as he was, in the boat. There were also other boats with him. A furious squall came up, and the waves broke over the boat, so that it was nearly swamped. Jesus was in the stern, sleeping on a cushion. The disciples woke him and said to him, 'Teacher, don't you care if we drown?' He got up, rebuked the wind and said to the waves, 'Quiet! Be still!' Then the wind died down and it was completely calm. He said to his disciples, 'Why are you so afraid? Do you still have no faith?' They were terrified and asked each other, 'Who is this? Even the wind and the waves obey him!'" (Mark 4:35-41).

"The Lord has established his throne in heaven, and his kingdom rules over all" (Psalm 103:19).

"God said to Moses, 'I AM WHO I AM. This is what you are to say to the Israelites: "I AM has sent me to you"'" (Exodus 3:14).

"The Lord will be king over the whole earth. On that day there will be one Lord, and his name the only name" (Zechariah 14:9).

Chapter Six

God *the Love*

It's my junior year in academy. Red Cross flyers cover our campus: little big-eyed girls plead for a chance to live, and white-capped nurses remind me that I, too, can save a life. *It won't take long,* the posters assure. *You'll be glad you did it. Make the world a better place.*

I sigh and walk back to an especially heartrending poster. I can't resist those little kids. I don't want to give an ounce of my blood, but I'll feel like a criminal if I refuse. So before I can change my mind, I borrow a pen and add my name to the growing list of donors.

On the Big Day, however, I'm not so sure I want to participate. I waver in the lobby of the gym, longing to run away from these needle-happy nurses.

"Step right over here." A claw-fingered woman grabs my shoulder and pushes me toward a table blanketed with consent forms. "Fill this out before you give your blood," she intones in a deep bass voice.

I nod and stare sullenly at the questionnaire. Blood drives always smell like disinfectant solution, and my stomach rebels.

"Finished?" Several minutes later the same nurse interrupts my thoughts with another shoulder-wrenching greeting. "Come over here to get your thumb pricked."

I draw back. "Am I giving blood through my thumb?"

"No," she cackles. "We just sample your blood for any reasons you can't be a donor."

"Oh."

Soon I'm sitting beside a plump woman who holds a nasty-looking instrument in her gloved fingers. "Hold out your thumb," she commands cheerfully.

I shut my eyes and obey. Suddenly a sharp sting makes me yelp. "Ouch!" A pool of blood appears on the ball of my thumb, and I resist the urge to slap this cruel woman.

"There now, that's the worst of it," she consoles. "The doctor will take care of you from here."

I slouch into the plastic seat and cross my arms. Beside me a boy laughs and talks, while streams of red liquid evacuate his body and enter a translucent bag overhead.

"Do you have to take that much blood?" I ask the doctor, pointing at my cheerful classmate. I picture my body shriveling up like an old balloon as the tube sucks my life away.

"Sure do."

I turn to him in disbelief, then gasp at the needle he holds poised over my arm.

My arm!

Before I can protest, the metal punctures my skin and a little mosquito-like machine starts sucking my blood away.

My blood!

I shut my eyes again, but the tears still come. I feel my identity, my strength, my very life leaving with that slender stream of blood.

"Are you all right?" The doctor leans anxiously over my chair.

"Just a little nervous," I quaver, staring up at his nostrils through blurry eyes. "I'll be f-f-f-f-fine."

I cry through the whole ordeal. Each time I think I've gained control, I glance at the slowly filling bag, and a fresh wave of panic sets in. *I don't care about those little kids!* I think ferociously. *My blood can't make a difference anyway. Just get me out of here!*

I haven't given blood since.

It's His last year on earth. Pain covers Jerusalem like a heavy woven blanket. Sin runs rampant in the streets, its consequences written in the faces of hungry children and tired old men.

It will feel like an eternity of hell, the tempter's voice assures Him. *And only a few will realize Your sacrifice.*

But He can't resist those hate-filled faces. Even the face of Judas holds a spot of value in His heart. His Father, watching from a distance, knows He will do it. The Spirit senses it too. They watch the drama unfurl like a bloodstained banner of victory.

He chooses to die.

He chooses the most horrible death that humans can invent. Willingly He adds His name to the list of the condemned.

"Are You in pain, Jesus?" they ask Him again and again. "Throw Yourself down from that cross. Save Yourself, if You can."

They don't know that it takes far more strength to stay than to go.

And He stays.

Alone on that cross, Jesus willingly gives His blood. His identity, His strength, His very life slips from His being in the ooze that quickens with every beat of His heart. Finally nothing remains but a broken body dangling from two crude pieces of wood.

Why? Why did a Father wish His own Son's death—let Him die for a near-hopeless cause—and their Spirit to forsake Him as He breathed His last tattered breath?

Because He can't resist us. None of Them can. They can't resist our poster-child eyes, the eyes of you and of me and of the wrath-filled ones who killed Him. We're all the same to Them, after all. All unworthy, yet somehow deserving of this great compassion They feel.

God *who*? Maybe now, after my own experience with blood, I can understand better. God the Love. The only—the strongest, the greatest—love this universe will ever know.

Reference Points:

"But God demonstrates his own love for us in this: While we were still sinners, Christ died for us" (Romans 5:8).

"How great is the love the Father has lavished on us, that we should be called children of God!" (1 John 3:1).

"Love never fails" (1 Corinthians 13:8).

"I am convinced that neither death nor life, neither angels nor demons, neither the present nor the future, nor any powers, neither height nor depth, nor anything else in all creation, will be able to separate us from the love of God that is in Christ Jesus our Lord" (Romans 8:38, 39).

"Greater love has no one than this, that he lay down his life for his friends" (John 15:13).

"He was pierced for our transgressions, he was crushed for our iniquities; the punishment that brought us peace was upon him, and by his wounds we are healed" (Isaiah 53:5).

"Let us fix our eyes on Jesus, the author and perfecter of our faith, who for the joy set before him endured the cross, scorning its shame, and sat down at the right hand of the throne of God" (Hebrews 12:2).

Chapter Seven

God *I Can Trust*

I slouch against the wall in my dorm's blue-carpeted hall with the phone receiver jammed against my right ear.

"What?" I interrupt Chris in the middle of a sentence, realizing I've been nearly asleep for the past five minutes.

"Oh, nothing. I was just telling you about my last physics test."

I grin. "I won't make you repeat yourself."

After a sleepy silence, I decide to bring up the topic I've been pondering for the past few weeks. "Chris, I've been thinking a lot about God," I begin tentatively.

"Yeah?" He sounds interested.

"Yeah." I pull on the phone cord. "I've been wondering how to trust Him. I mean, I can't just snap my fingers and have an incredible faith."

"I know." Chris's voice fades momentarily, and I can almost see him scrunching down in the tiny phone booth in his fraternity for a long conversation. "I've been wondering the same thing. Where do we start?"

"You mean, you don't have the answer?" I joke.

He sighs, sending a puff of noise through countless telephone connections and into my ear. "I wish I did. It probably starts when a person is born again."

Born again. My mind wanders back to the faded square pictures in my baby book. In one frame a girl holds a tiny bundle of life and smiles tiredly at the camera. In another the girl's husband holds the same bundle, carefully, as though it might shatter at any instant. In the third picture the bundle lies alone in an incubator, wrapped in a soft yellow blanket, with a too-big bracelet on a pudgy pink arm. *Sarah Coleman,* the label reads.

Each time I glance through those pictures my own name surprises me. That red face is mine! Those high school kids are my parents! Though I know it's true, I can scarcely believe my eyes.

Born again.

Somehow our family survived the weeks following my birth. As tired as they were, Mom and Dad kept me warm, dry, and well-fed—the basic needs of life. Beyond that, they gave me love—the basic need for a happy life.

"Chris!" My voice startles us both.

"What did you think of?"

"Let's see if this works." My words jumble together in my excitement. "We compare God to our earthly father or mother, right?"

"Yeah."

"Think about your own parents. How did you begin trusting them?"

Chris's laugh rolls easily into my ear. "I don't know. It just happened. They took me home from the hospital and fed me and kept me warm—"

"Exactly!" I blurt out. "They took care of your basic needs. And even though you were too little to understand, that built up a trust in your mind. Right?"

"Yeah. So?"

"As time went on, you realized that they wouldn't stop. Your trust probably grew stronger. Pretty soon you picked up on the fact that they loved you. They *wanted* to take care of you."

"Yeah . . ." Comprehension creeps into Chris's voice.

"And by the time you were old enough to make sense out of everything, you knew your parents would feed you and love you and do everything they could to make you happy." I pause. "Because you trusted them with the basics as a baby, that trust sort of grew up with you."

"You know what? This makes sense!" I can almost hear his smile. "It's so easy to apply that to—"

"God."

No wonder the Bible uses the phrase *born again*. It's the easiest analogy for humans to understand. Not only does new birth signify new life, but it applies to the strengthening of our faith as well.

I began trusting Mom and Dad before I knew what I was doing. I opened my mouth, and food poured in. It was inexplicably simple.

Somewhere, sometime before I even realized it, I began the same way with God. I opened my eyes, and my heart started beating. I breathed in, and my lungs functioned properly. I swallowed, and my food went down the right tube. I lived.

My earthly parents made me happy. Before I knew how to ask, they presented me with cuddly blankets, colorful toys, and enough attention for three babies. They loved to make me smile.

Before I realized what He was doing, my other Parent made me happy as well. He lavished sunshine, green grass, and bird songs on my days. He sent close friends and unexpected blessings my way. His efforts to make me smile equaled those of my parents on earth.

Next I learned that when I cried, my parents would make things better. I cried when I awoke hungry in the night. They fed me. I cried when my diaper was dirty. They changed it. I cried when I grew sick or tired. They soothed me, loved me, and nestled me down to sleep. Sometimes they noticed a problem even before I told them about it. And always they fixed it.

With my heavenly Parent I'm learning the same lesson. When I'm discouraged, He gives me strength. When I'm lonely, His companionship outshines all the others'. When I'm afraid, He calms my fears or dispels the danger. Sometimes He notices a problem even before I tell Him about it. And always He fixes it.

Born again? Yes, I think that fits the process of my growing faith. I don't need to snap my fingers and create an instant trust in God. In fact, I don't even want to. I like this method much better. I like building on a faith I didn't know I had. I like realizing that before I knew enough to struggle for it, my trust was already forming for this Parent I'm getting to know.

It's a great feeling. And like the faith I have in my parents, I know it will grow.

God *who*? The God I can trust. The God I've trusted already in the shadowy corners of my heart. The God I trust more each day.

Reference Points:

"He said: 'I tell you the truth, unless you change and become like little children, you will never enter the kingdom of heaven'" (Matthew 18:3).

"Praise be to the Lord, to God our Savior, who daily bears our burdens" (Psalm 68:19).

"It is better to take refuge in the Lord than to trust in man" (Psalm 118:8).

"Like newborn babies, crave pure spiritual milk, so that by it you may grow up in your salvation, now that you have tasted that the Lord is good" (1 Peter 2:2, 3).

Chapter Eight

God I Must Trust

I've always been afraid of streams. I know it's unreasonable, but that doesn't change the feeling I get every time I step on a log laid across a rushing current. I start out bravely, not mentioning to anyone that I'm afraid I'll end up underneath the log.

It's not that swift, I assure myself. *Just don't look down.* I keep my head up and my eyes focused on the neck of the person in front of me. But inevitably my common sense prevails. *You've got to look down!* my mind insists. *This log is wet and slimy, and for all you know, you could be about to step on a patch of loose bark.*

That ends my courageous streak. One glance at the rushing water paralyzes me completely. I freeze on that log as quickly as though someone had just spread Super Glue on the soles of my shoes. Only the knowledge that I don't want to spend the rest of my life standing over all that water can make me move again.

Nothing is different on this backpacking trip.

"Sarah, hurry up!" Angie's voice interrupts my bumbling progress through the trees.

"Why?" I mumble, brushing a wet spider web from my face. "It's already dark." While we roasted marshmallows earlier that evening, the sun slipped beneath the mountains and left our forest in mosquito-singing shadows.

"Are you sure this is a good idea?" I ask for the thirtieth time.

"Of course it is!" Ahead of me, Angie branch-snaps her way toward the stream. "You thought of it, remember?"

"Yeah, but that was before—" I shake my head. It's no use. In a moment of inspiration I'd suggested a pilgrimage to The Other Side for the night. Only afterward had I remembered that mountain streams don't come equipped with concrete bridges.

"Oops!" Angie's voice, accompanied by a *slide-splash* sound reaches my ears. "I found the water! And hey, here's a log, too!"

"Great." I mumble, following the trail to the place where she stands by a fallen tree. "Oh. Oh, no!"

"What?"

I gaze across the wide expanse of white water. "Uh . . ."

"Oh, that's right." Angie giggles. "You hate this part." She lifts one leg onto the log. "Well, don't worry. It's a big tree, and— Whoa! Guess it's rotten. Watch for loose bark." Her voice blends with the rush of the current as she walks away. Her arms and legs protrude around her backpack, giving her the look of a gigantic tightrope-walking beetle.

I heist my first leg onto the log. "Well, don't worry . . ." I mimic her carefree expression. "Easy for *you* to say."

A movement across the stream catches my attention. It's Angie, waving her arms like a windmill in a tornado, encouraging me to hurry.

I shudder. "I'm coming, I'm coming!" As one step turns into two, three, and four, I keep up a steady dialogue with myself. *Two more steps to the branch. Catch your balance. One . . . two . . . Ease around it, and keep going—* Let go of the branch first! *And don't look down!*

Immediately my gaze shifts. The stream rushes beneath me like a freeway packed with angry white cars. The weight of my full backpack could easily pull me off my perch. I picture myself hitting the water face first and clawing to the surface for air. *My pack will hold me under!*

"Stop it, Sarah!" I wrench my eyes upward and focus on the next sturdy limb. "You've got to keep moving!" But when I try to lift my feet, I can't budge. The inevitable has happened. Again. My knees begin shaking, and I feel sick to my stomach. *It's so far down!* The persistent image of my fall from the log flashes across my brain like a strobe light. I crouch on the log and grasp a big knot with both hands. *I can't fall in if I'm not moving!* I think grimly.

"Sarah!" Angie's voice sounds from above.

I look up at her and attempt a smile. "Why are you here?"

She holds out a grubby hand. "Hold on," she commands sternly. "And stand up."

I obediently stand—but not up. I can't bring myself to relinquish my hold on that precious knot. My backpack threatens to topple me facefirst into the stream.

"Give me your hand," Angie yells above the noise, "and we'll cross it together."

I shake my head and remove one of my hands from the knot. "I'll pull you in with me. Go back to shore."

"I'm not moving. And I'm *not* falling in." She stretches her arm a little closer. "Just grab on."

"I can't!" The strobe light picture now includes Angie, pulled off the log by a top-heavy Sarah. "Go back!"

"I won't." Angie holds her ground. Ignoring her, I pull my other hand free of the knot and stand up straight. *This is silly,* I tell myself. *I know I can do it alone.*

"Do you trust me?" Once again Angie's voice surprises me.

"Yes, Angie," I sigh. "Now go back to shore. I'll be just—"

"Then *grab my hand.*" Her argument stops me cold.

"I trust you," I repeat. "It's *me* I don't trust. I'll pull us both in." I appraise my knot on the log, wondering if it could support my entire weight.

"I won't fall in. I've done it once already, remember? Just trust me, Sarah."

"No . . ." But my resolve weakens. After several more arguments, I meekly grab her hand, and we begin moving. As our journey progresses, I grow more sure of my steps. After all, I can see Angie's feet directly in front of me. If she can do it, so can I.

"That wasn't so bad, was it?" We jump to the ground and Angie releases my hand. I plop down hard on the sandy beach.

What seemed like an ordinary trip across an ordinary log to Angie had been a nearly fatal experience for me—until I grabbed her hand. I sit on the beach for a long time, oblivious to the moisture soaking through the seat of my sweatpants.

Do you trust me? Angie's question echoes through my memory. *Of course I trust Angie. She's my best friend. I just didn't want to pull her into the water with me. I was being unselfish and—*

I won't fall in. I've done it once already. Her argument stops my thoughts again.

I trust her, I argue to myself. *I've just never been on a rotten log over a swollen stream on a cloudy night with her—and wearing a three-ton backpack, no less. Yeah, I trust her. I've just never had to trust her with my survival.*

I shiver, suddenly aware of the night chill and the mosquitoes feasting on my bare arms. "Hey, Ang!" I call in the direction of her fuzzy shadow. "Let's get that tarp set up. It's freezing out here!"

Do you trust Me?

How often has Christ asked me that question, stretching His hand toward my crouching form? I perch alone on a log of fear and pain with the waters of despair rushing beneath my feet.

I don't want any company right now, God, I insist. *I can handle this by myself. Sure, I'm scared to take another step. But I'll be fine. I don't want to drag You through this with me.*

He reaches a little closer. *I won't fall in. I've done this once already, remember?*

No, no. I shake my head and try to stand alone, the pressure of my life nearly toppling me into the water. *Just go back to the shore.*

Do you trust Me?

I wipe the tears from my face and try to smile. *Sure, Lord. But I've never actually had to give You my life before. I mean, this is a little different than your average problem.*

Yes, I know. Take My hand.

But— My resolve starts to crumble as I watch that steady hand open toward my own. He's done it before.

We won't fall. I promise. He looks deep into my soul, and I reach toward that hand stretched out in the darkness.

In an instant our palms meet and He pulls me to my feet. *Let's go!*

As I follow Him across that dizzying stream, I feel the raised outline of a scar where a nail once punctured His hand.

I've done it all before.

Do you trust Him?

Reference Points:

"Even youths grow tired and weary, and young men stumble and fall; but those who hope in the Lord will renew their strength. They will soar on wings like eagles; they will run and not grow weary, they will walk and not be faint" (Isaiah 40:30, 31).

"I trust in your unfailing love; my heart rejoices in your salvation" (Psalm 13:5).

"Trust in the Lord with all your heart and lean not on your own understanding; in all your ways acknowledge him, and he will make your paths straight" (Proverbs 3:5, 6).

Chapter Nine

God the Silent

It was only one ride. But to me it was life and death.

"Come on, Sarah. You know you want to do it!" Joie's sunny blue eyes searched my face.

"I do?" I stared doubtfully at the monster before us.

"Yeah!" she encouraged. "It's a blast. I've been on it three times already."

Beside her, Braden nodded. "It's true. She's a maniac."

"I know." I grinned ruefully. Joie, my roommate during our senior year in academy, constantly surprised me with her outrageous antics. "And I'm not sure I want to go with her!"

"Sarah!" Joie groaned and stomped her foot. "Please? Please, just for me? You'll regret it for the rest of your life if you don't. *Please?"* She knelt, grabbed my hand, and stared beseechingly up at me.

Studiously ignoring my friend, I gazed around Edmonton Mall's crowded amusement park. Everywhere I turned, I spotted someone I knew. During this, our senior class trip, the place was dotted with familiar faces. Would I regret not trying the Mind Bender? I stared up at its towering track and shivered.

"Come on, Sarah." Braden took Joie's side. "Conquer your worst fear!"

That did it. "All right," I agreed. "I'll go."

"Great!" Joie grabbed me and jerked me into line. "Sarah, you and I are sitting in the very front car."

"Why?" We inched forward behind a large man already breathing heavily with excitement.

"Because it's the scariest!"

Before I could protest, a harried attendant moved us to the front car, strapped our safety belts on, and disappeared into the crowd.

"Wait!" I called after her, clawing at my safety belt. "I don't want to be here!"

"Oh, you'll be fine." Braden, sitting in the car behind us, consoled me. "Just hold on and enjoy the ride."

"Thanks," I growled, glaring at Joie.

She grinned and settled into her seat. "Here we go!"

"Aaaaaauuuughhhh!" My scream of pure terror started the ride with a bang. Even though our car was merely chugging up a steep incline, I knew we'd have a drop on the other side. On every side mirrors and lights gave the ride an otherworldly look.

"I can't do this! I can't do this! I can't do this!" I screamed over and over, clenching my fingers around Joie's left arm. "Stop the car! Help me! *Stop the car!"*

But Joie remained silent. And still we inched upward. Slowly, slowly, the car crested the top of the incline. A maze of tracks and metal stabilizers spread below us like an iron spider's death trap.

Without warning we dropped into the nightmare below. Around bends, through tunnels, in crazy loops and turns, our car careened. From the cars behind I heard sounds of pleased surprise. But my own voice grew hoarse from terrified screams. Still Joie didn't speak.

"Help me! Oh, God, help me! Help me! Joie, why did you do this! *Aaaaauuugh!* Help me!" Finally, too worn out to care, I slumped in my seat and let my head flop from side to side. "I'm going to die!" I called to Joie as we twisted upside down on a corner. "I know I'm going to die."

She merely smiled and pointed ahead to the next loop. I closed my eyes and awaited my fate. *Whooosh!* The airy sound of a whistle jarred my mind. My eyes eased open.

"Are you getting out?" the same frazzled attendant asked, her face inches from my own.

"Wha— Huh?" I blinked and focused on her nose.

"Are you getting out? Ride's over, lady."

"Come on!" Joie laughed. She reached in and helped me from the car. "That wasn't so bad, was it?"

Braden stood beside her, grinning as though he'd thoroughly enjoyed himself. His smile blurred, and I blinked again. He reached out to steady me.

"Yes," I quavered. "Yes, it *was* bad." And I sat down right there on the cement floor and cried. I was alive! I had known beyond the tiniest doubt that I would die. Yet here I was, sobbing and hiccuping on the same floor I had left five minutes before. It was all too much to handle.

"Wh-wh-why did you take me on that?" I finally stuttered to Joie, who had plopped down cross-legged in front of me. "And why didn't you answer me when I screamed?"

Again Joie flashed me that mischievous grin. "Don't worry. You'll thank me later."

At the time, gratitude was the furthest thing from my mind. But now, two years down the road, I can honestly say I'm glad I conquered the Mind Bender. Every other roller coaster is tame in comparison. I can relax (sort of) and enjoy almost any ride I come across—all because Joie took me on the world-famous Mind Bender.

You'll thank Me later. Countless times I've felt the same frustration with God. In the middle of a nightmarish experience, I call aloud for deliverance.

Nothing happens.

I struggle to survive, positive that I can never conquer the temptation I face.

He doesn't rescue me.

I scream for mercy when my strength stretches to its tightest.

I feel no relief.

Why, when I need Him the most, does God often remain silent? How can a God of love leave me dangling at the end of a slowly tightening hangman's noose? I, like David, look to the hills and ask,

"Where does my help come from?" (Psalm 121:1). And all too often those hills don't reply. Is God asleep? Snoozing on the job of saving an insignificant world? David didn't think so!

"My help comes from the Lord, the Maker of heaven and earth. He will not let your foot slip—He who watches over you will not slumber. . . . The Lord will watch over your coming and going both now and forevermore" (Psalm 121:2-8).

These words remind me of what I should already know. Just as I trusted Joie to steer clear of dangerous rides, so I trust God. "And God is faithful; he will not let you be tempted beyond what you can bear" (1 Corinthians 10:13). Whether I hear His assurances or not, I know that He's in control of my existence. And like Joie, He won't send me out alone; He's always right beside me. This alone can comfort me when I yell for help and hear no response. Even though He may remain silent, I know that later I truly will thank my God for the experience we share.

Reference Points:

"Those who suffer he delivers in their suffering; he speaks to them in their affliction" (Job 36:15).

"I am always with you; you hold me by my right hand. You guide me with your counsel, and afterward you will take me into glory" (Psalm 73:23, 24).

"I, the Lord, have called you in righteousness; I will take hold of your hand" (Isaiah 42:6).

"O Lord, you have seen this; be not silent. Do not be far from me, O Lord. Awake, and rise to my defense!" (Psalm 35:22, 23).

Chapter Ten

God *of the Lost*

(Based on Deuteronomy 32:48-52 and 34)

"Milk and honey," He said. "I'll give you a land flowing with milk and honey."

I have to admit, those words sounded mighty tempting after wandering around the scrubby hills of Goshen for 40 years. I pictured the slow sweet waves of honey, and the milk flowing in rivers. I hadn't tasted honey since I left the palace. I hadn't drunk cool milk in years.

His offer sounded so tantalizing that I agreed to the responsibility that came with it. He wanted me to lead those Hebrews to the Promised Land. I'd have to hike on back to Egypt and convince that black-hearted king to let his prime source of income scramble to the wilderness. Forever. My prospects for success weren't exactly promising.

But I had to try. After 40 years alone with those sheep, anything sounded better than another day of finding water and pasture for ungrateful beasts.

Good ol' Pharaoh. He hated me the moment he saw me. I knew Yahweh would have to do some pretty slick tricks to rescue my persecuted people.

My people. Yes, they were mine, and I was theirs. For all my high education and refined ways, I really was one of them. My mother, Jochebed, bore me in fear that the slave drivers would drown me. Imagine her surprise when instead they asked to raise me at the palace! I became arrogant then, and lorded it over my own family as if I were their superior.

But Yahweh took that mean streak clear out of me. Took Him 40 years to convince me I wasn't Pharaoh's gift to the kingdom, but He finally did. I started eating with the humble folks and enjoying their simple lives. And just when I thought I had settled down for good, Yahweh came along with this job offer . . .

But I was telling you about our trip to the palace.

Aaron and I stayed quite some time in Egypt, trying to convince the hospitable Pharaoh to give us his Hebrews. Of course it didn't work, so Yahweh stepped in with a few miracles. Frogs, dust, gnats, grasshoppers—He sent so many creepy crawly things at those Egyptians that pretty soon they were creeping and crawling too.

"Take them," they begged. "Take those cursed Hebrews and leave our country at once!"

We were only too eager to comply.

I could go on and on about the journey. I could tell you about the chase to the Red Sea and the stink of the soldiers' rotting bodies after they drowned. I could tell you about the party on the other side, and the cloud that kept us safe. I could list all the battles we fought and describe the fear in strangers' eyes when they heard who our God was. But that would take too long.

I'll just tell you that no matter what anyone says, herding people is a whole lot tougher than herding sheep. I've never seen a more confusing group of individuals in my life. First they begged for food. And then, when Yahweh gave it to them, they begged for meat. They couldn't stay satisfied for two sunny days in a row. They bickered over donkeys, over tent space, and even over whom they had to travel with. I tried to explain that Yahweh would bring them to a wonderful land—milk, honey, the whole bit—but they got so tired of my story they accused me of making it all up.

I remember the time I climbed the mountain to talk with Yahweh about the rules and laws He'd instated. Well, when I returned, those Hebrews were all worshiping a big golden cow! I almost quit right then and there. *Yahweh,* I remember thinking, *we've been roaming this desert for years. I'm tired of apologizing for these stiff-necked people. I'm tired of settling their squabbles.*

But the journey went on. Some days the dust stung my eyes so badly I went sand blind. Other days the sun shone down all yellowy-white, as if it wanted to kill us all. And sometimes that pillar of cloud kept right on moving far into the night. And of course we followed it. We would have been lost in this unfamiliar land without it.

And do you know what? After 20 years of groaning and fighting and sand in my bed, Yahweh told me we had another 20 coming. He said it was because of the people being so hard-hearted.

Well, you can imagine their joy when I told them that one. You know, some of them didn't make it to the Promised Land. The old ones died before they got a chance to see those spring-green valleys all jeweled with dew. We buried them right where they died, alone, in the scrub hills.

It bothers me when I think about it. All those whining, bickering people, and only about half the original crowd getting to see their land. Sure, I got upset at them sometimes. But when we finally got to the border, I realized I was actually thankful that Yahweh had brought me through that wilderness with them. I realized I loved them. It made it hard to say goodbye.

Oh, I forgot to tell you about that. You see, I'm no better than any one of them. I kept taking this journey into my own hands and messing things up. Finally, because of my lack of faith, Yahweh told me I could not enter the Promised Land.

He asked me to climb this mountain today. He told me I wouldn't come down again. So I said my goodbyes as quickly as I could and set out up that slope in a straight line to the summit. I tried not to look back too often, but every time I did, I saw that little girl. She wore a faded red robe and a strange sort of smile, as though we shared some special secret. Finally I lost her in the crowd. When I turned away the last time, I felt a wetness on my face. Tears.

Yes, I'll miss those complaining Hebrews. But I don't think I'll miss them for long. You see, Yahweh asked me to climb this mountain. He said I would die up here with a great view of the Promised Land below me. But to tell you the truth, I wouldn't have minded dying right there on the valley floor.

No, I'm not discouraged. Of course I wish I could continue the journey with my people. But I'm ready to die if Yahweh says it's time.

I am an old man, and I have walked many miles. Now that this journey is complete, I am tired of walking . . . What? Oh, the milk an honey. Well, the funniest thing happened. Somewhere between pleading with the people to honor Yahweh and pleading with Yahweh to protect the people, I sort of forgot about that. I forgot that the milk and the honey were my original reason for starting this trip. Somehow I forgot to concentrate on the destination and focused on the journey instead. Each sunrise I woke up and saw that big tall cloud, and I knew Yahweh would lead us exactly where He wanted us to go. I didn't worry so much about where that might be. Instead, I got kind of satisfied with wandering, because I knew that Yahweh wouldn't let us stay lost in the wilderness forever.

It was a nice feeling. Now, even though I know my God is a God of exotic destinations, I am just as content with the journey. For it is in the journey that I came to know Him best—my God, the God of the lost.

Reference Points:

"Whether you turn to the right or to the left, your ears will hear a voice behind you, saying, 'This is the way; walk in it'" (Isaiah 30:21).

"When he has tested me, I will come forth as gold. My feet have closely followed his steps; I have kept to his way without turning aside. I have not departed from the commands of his lips; I have treasured the words of his mouth more than my daily bread" (Job 23:10-12).

"It is God who arms me with strength and makes my way perfect. He makes my feet like the feet of a deer; he enables me to stand on the heights" (Psalm 18:32, 33).

"Let the morning bring me word of your unfailing love, for I have put my trust in you. Show me the way I should go" (Psalm 143:8).

"In his heart a man plans his course, but the Lord determines his steps" (Proverbs 16:9).

"To this you were called, because Christ suffered for you, leaving you an example, that you should follow in his steps" (1 Peter 2:21).

Chapter Eleven

God *of Grace*

"So, what is it?" a friend queried as we sat in my writer's cabin and held our snow-cold feet inches from my tiny heater.

"Grace? Uh—" My mind spun in circles. Nobody had asked me a question like that before.

"Is it like never falling or something? Does 'God's grace' mean God is really coordinated?"

I couldn't help smiling at the definition, but I knew I couldn't provide anything better. I'd been a Christian my entire life, and I still couldn't describe a word as simple as "grace"? It didn't even have five syllables!

After that night I made it my personal mission to discover the meaning of grace. Back at college I jumped headlong into the rush of assignments and friends, but I kept the question always in mind. And though I don't remember the exact moment "grace" became a powerful word in my vocabulary, I do recall the moment grace made its biggest impact on me.

By the time we performed the skit, I was well aware that grace meant God's love and forgiveness, regardless of our character. But the skit Cory and I performed brought that realization down to a raw personal level.

"Can you think up something to do for tonight's

InTents meeting?" Jen, our drama director, asked me. "I've done the last two skits, and I'm sure the audience would like a change."

I nodded automatically. How hard could it be to create a two-minute skit? "What time should I be there?"

"Oh, 6:15 or so." She hefted her book bag to her shoulder. "See you there. And thanks again."

"No problem."

No problem? A half hour later I realized just what a problem this skit might be. Although I enjoyed any opportunity to create new dramas, my mind drew a blank when I begged it for ideas.

Grace. Suddenly that one word sparked my imagination. Why not make a drama with grace, the theme of my thoughts lately, as its center? It would take only two characters. . . .

That evening the InTents meeting was fuller than usual. Cory and I stepped into position.

Scene one. "Jesus?" I began in a high singsong voice. "Jesus, are You there? Good. 'Cause I'm not ready to go to sleep. Mommy says I have to, but . . ." I continued the first monologue glibly. I was a little girl listing her shortcomings to Jesus. "And I promise I'll never pull the cat's tail again," I concluded proudly.

Cory, playing the part of Jesus, smiled at me and looked to heaven. "Father, forgive her. She is the perfect picture of innocence."

Scene two. "Jesus?" I began again, pacing the stage. "Jesus, can You hear me? I've got some questions for You." This time I represented a lost, searching individual. "Where are You?" I repeated again and again.

Beside me, "Jesus" waved His arms and snapped His fingers in my face. I didn't see Him.

"All right," I finally concluded. "If that's the way You want to be, I guess I can't believe in You. There's just not enough evidence."

"Jesus" looked to the sky. "Father, forgive her, for she is searching for her faith."

Last scene. "Jesus? Jesus, why did You let this happen? He was so young, so innocent!" Now I played the part of a grief-racked woman who had lost a relative to AIDS. "Did You do this on purpose, Jesus?" I sneered at Him.

He turned His face, as though I'd hit Him.

"You did, didn't You? Well, I hate You for what You've done to my life. I hate You! I hate You! I hate You!" My words pounded "Jesus" to the cross. Louder, louder I screamed. Deeper, deeper, drove the imaginary nails. Finally I collapsed, sobbing, at His feet.

"Jesus" bent and wrapped His arms around my shaking body. "Father, forgive her. She doesn't know what she's doing," He pleaded to the sky.

As Cory and I walked offstage amid the crowd's applause, I held his arm for support.

"Good job!" he congratulated me. "That was awesome!"

"Cory, my legs are still shaking!" I whispered in awe.

Something about this drama impacted me more deeply than any dictionary definition of grace. Perhaps it was because each scene represented, to some degree, a different time in my life. Perhaps it was the knowledge that no matter what I did to Him—even to the point of death—Jesus would always love me. Never before had I felt that surety in such a concrete form. And though it left me trembling and close to tears, I loved it.

Grace? Grace, to me, is visible in those three scenes Cory and I performed.

The forgiveness God gives to simple believers.

The forgiveness He extends to doubting searchers.

The forgiveness He offers to those who rage against His name, asking no pardon for their actions.

God *who*? God, a God of grace, so much grace that it touches even those, like me, who kill Him with their sins.

Reference Points:

"He said to me, 'My grace is sufficient for you, for my power is made perfect in weakness'" (2 Corinthians 12:9).

"From the fullness of his grace we have all received one blessing after another" (John 1:16).

"All have sinned and fall short of the glory of God, and are justified freely by his grace through the redemption that came by Christ Jesus" (Romans 3:23, 24).

"He chose us in him before the creation of the world to be holy and blameless in his sight. In love he predestined us to be adopted as his sons through Jesus Christ, in accordance with his pleasure and will—to the praise of his glorious grace, which he has freely given us in the One he loves. In him we have redemption through his blood, the forgiveness of sins, in accordance with the riches of God's grace that he lavished on us with all wisdom and understanding" (Ephesians 1:4-8).

"It is by grace you have been saved, through faith—and this not from yourselves, it is the gift of God—not by works, so that no one can boast" (Ephesians 2:8, 9)

"The grace of our Lord was poured out on me abundantly, along with the faith and love that are in Christ Jesus. Here is a trustworthy saying that deserves full acceptance: Christ Jesus came into the world to save sinners—of whom I am the worst. But for that very reason I was shown mercy so that in me, the worst of sinners, Christ Jesus might display his unlimited patience as an example for those who would believe on him and receive eternal life" (1 Timothy 1:14-16).

Chapter Twelve

God *of Peace*

A rustle moves through the grass.
Awake in an instant, the boy opens his eyes to the night. Blackness meets him like a wall, and for a moment he wonders if he has gone suddenly blind. *Where did that rustle come from?*

As his pupils adjust, he recognizes the shadows of his father's sleeping sheep. *The rustle! Where is it?*

The sheep stand in scraggly clumps among the low bushes of this unprotected plain.

Through the grass, the rustle moves again.

Every muscle tense, David eases from his bedroll and crouches in the dark.

What is it this time? A lion? A bear? Or something bigger? His mind draws pictures of huge creatures, their teeth bared against him.

"Where are you?" David whispers into the night. He clutches his sling in one hand, and a crude stone-headed spear in the other.

David senses the movement almost before he hears it. In one fluid motion he turns and leaps forward to face the giant.

Nothing! His flailing arms meet yielding blackness. The rustle continues, somehow behind him again. "Ahhh." David lets his pent-up yell of attack escape in a whooshing sigh. "Only the wind. Again." Thankful no humans witnessed his drama, David returns to his now-cold bedroll and tries to sleep.

But sleep will not come. Instead, memories of his first lion torment his mind. Only a boy at the time, he hadn't realized the danger of his actions. "Die!" he'd yelled at the beast's snarling face. "Die for killing my father's sheep!"

And it had died. A great rotting carcass, it had lain in that forsaken valley until its bones bleached white in the sun. Each time he brought the flock home, he passed that spot and remembered the fight.

He rubs the scar that runs the length of his forearm, lost in the memories. This lion had been only the first in a long succession of predators that summer. And alone with his sling, he'd killed them all.

He sighs and reaches under his blanket to remove a troublesome rock. *They may be dead these two years, but these beasts have left me their memories. I cannot slay a memory.* Slowly, fitfully, he drifts off to sleep as the sheep stir and shuffle on the plain.

Before the lions came David had been a carefree shepherd, alone with his music and his flock. But something in those experiences tainted his outlook with a suspicion he couldn't ignore. Behind every bush lurked a predator; in every valley waited an unexpected threat. David acquired the shifty-eyed look of a seasoned herdsman, something he'd vowed he'd never have.

But it couldn't be helped. These images from the past were too strong to conquer. Even in moments of perfect safety they haunted him. Danger seemed a tangible thing to evade, and peace an equally tangible object to pursue.

If only . . . he sometimes thought as he sat alone by the fire. *If only I could shake these fears and live again with the peace I used to feel.*

Slowly, slowly, through the music that brought him closest to that peace, David began to find an answer. *I have forgotten You for so long,* he mused as he played. *Yet You protect me still.*

And then the songs began to emerge. Full and courageous, a challenge to those beasts of the past, he sang them.

> How long must I wrestle with my thoughts
> and every day have sorrow in my heart?

Do not be far from me,
for trouble is near
and there is no one to help.

Turn to me and be gracious to me,
for I am lonely and afflicted.
The troubles of my heart have multiplied;
free me from all my anguish.

Contend, O Lord, with those who contend with me;
fight against those who fight against me.
Take up shield and buckler;
arise and come to my aid.
Brandish spear and javelin
against those who pursue me.
Say to my soul,
"I am your salvation."

Guard my life and rescue me;
let me not be put to shame,
for I take refuge in You.

I will take refuge in the shadow of Your wings
until the disaster has passed.

I will lie down and sleep in peace,
for You alone, O Lord,
make me dwell in safety.

My heart is steadfast, O God:
I will sing and make music with all my soul.
Awake, harp and lyre!
I will awaken the dawn.

My soul finds rest in God alone.

—Psalms 13:2; 22:11; 25:16, 17;
35:1-3; 25:20; 4:8; 37:1, 2; 62:1

God *who*? God of a peace deep enough to conquer even the strongest of fears, the deepest of pain. God of a peace steadfast enough to calm wind and waves and worries in one command. God of a peace big enough to cover David; a peace big enough to cover me; a peace big enough to cover the whole restless world.

Reference Points:

"Peace I leave with you; my peace I give you. I do not give to you as the world gives. Do not let your hearts be troubled and do not be afraid" (John 14:27).

"The God of peace will soon crush Satan under your feet. The grace of our Lord Jesus be with you" (Romans 16:20).

"Great peace have they who love your law, and nothing can make them stumble" (Psalm 119:165).

"You will keep in perfect peace him whose mind is steadfast, because he trusts in you" (Isaiah 26:3).

"You will go out in joy and be led forth in peace; the mountains and hills will burst into song before you, and all the trees of the field will clap their hands" (Isaiah 55:12).

"The peace of God, which transcends all understanding, will guard your hearts and your minds in Christ Jesus" (Philippians 4:7).

"Peacemakers who sow in peace raise a harvest of righteousness" (James 3:18).

Chapter Thirteen

God *Who (More Than) Conquers*

"How . . . do . . . you . . . feel?" I ask Caroline between gasps for air.

"Sweaty!" Her feet pound in perfect rhythm with mine on the sizzling-hot highway. I wheeze out a laugh and focus my attention on an upcoming hill. *Breathe in, four steps, breathe out, four steps, breathe in, four steps . . . How much farther can I run?*

Caroline and I have trained together since Christmas. Today, track and field day for our academy, is a perfect opportunity to test our endurance against the grueling road race to Liberty High School.

"Let's . . . speed . . . up!" Caroline suggests as we crest the hill. "We're almost there."

I look up and spot the high school ahead. Crowds of academy students mill around the track. My legs scream in protest as we accelerate. *Breathe in, four steps, breathe out* . . . My body begs for more oxygen, and I feel the familiar tightening of my throat that signals an asthmatic attack. *Ignore it!*

My noisy breathing sounds like a dying steam engine, but I refuse to stop and rest. I can see the finish line ahead—will I die before I get there? *You can do this, Sarah! Just a little farther. Breathe in, one step, breathe out, one step, breathe in . . . breathe!*

I sense bright colors and cheering friends but can't look up to acknowledge them. Each step on the crumbly track sounds unforgettably clear in my pounding ears. *Breathe! Step! Breathe!*

Just when I think my body will fall to pieces, I cross the finish line and collapse on the grass, gasping for breath. Immediately a crowd of friends surrounds me. Someone pulls me to the water station, and I let the cool liquid soothe my parched throat.

"You did it, Sarah!"

"Congratulations!"

"I can't believe you kept running! Are you OK?"

Comments fly thick above my head, but I can't reply. Laughing and crying all at once, I look over at Caroline. Our eyes meet in mutual understanding, and I know that no matter where I place in the final standings, I've completely conquered this race.

The memory of this experience surfaces a year later as I sit in a discussion group at college. Broc, an enthusiastic member of our group, presents us with a problem.

"I've been thinking about this verse all day," he confesses. His blue eyes search our faces. "And it still bothers me. What on earth is Paul talking about?"

"Well," pipes up Caroline, who shares the leadership of the group with me, "it might help if we knew what verse you're talking about!"

Amid a ripple of laughter, Broc sheepishly opens his Bible. "Right here, Romans 8:37: 'In all these things we are more than conquerors through him who loved us.'" He looks up in confusion. "I understand how a person can conquer something, but how do you *more than* conquer? It doesn't make sense."

"Maybe," Scott begins, "it means doing more than what's necessary to conquer something. Putting everything you've got into being victorious."

I nod, remembering the effort it took for Caroline and me to complete that race to Liberty High. "Even though it's not always fun, it's worth it at the end of the race, right?"

Broc nods. "Yeah, I can see that. But I'm supposed to be *more than* a conqueror in everything I do. What if I fail?"

"You're never a failure if you've honestly done your best,"

Caroline reminds him quietly. "I think God measures success by something bigger than gold medals."

I think Caroline's right. I can picture Him now, greeting us at the gates of heaven as we enter for the very first time. "Good job! Congratulations! I'm so proud of you for finishing! Way to go!"

I know being a conqueror won't be fun all the time, but if I keep this picture in my mind, I'll remember that it will all be worthwhile when the race is over.

God. My God, the Conqueror. The one who knows all about struggle and stress, pain and practice. The one who watches as we run this race, eager for the opportunity to congratulate us at the finish line. The one who has (more than) conquered the race already.

Reference Points:

"Let us throw off everything that hinders and the sin that so easily entangles, and let us run with perseverance the race marked out for us. Let us fix our eyes on Jesus, the author and perfecter of our faith, who for the joy set before him endured the cross, scorning its shame, and sat down at the right hand of the throne of God. Consider him who endured such opposition from sinful men, so that you will not grow weary and lose heart" (Hebrews 12:1-3).

"I have told you these things, so that in me you may have peace. In this world you will have trouble. But take heart! I have overcome the world" (John 16:33).

"In all these things we are more than conquerors through him who loved us" (Romans 8:37).

"Do you not know that in a race all the runners run, but only one gets the prize? Run in such a way as to get the prize. Everyone who competes in the games goes into strict training. They do it to get a crown that will not last; but we do it to get a crown that will last forever. Therefore I do not run like a man running aimlessly; I do not fight like a man beating the air. No, I beat my body and make it my slave so that after I have preached to others, I myself will not be disqualified for the prize" (1 Corinthians 9:24-27).

Chapter Fourteen

God *I Can Talk To*

You know who I am. You've just never seen me take this form before.

You thought I must be restricted to silence, but I am not a secret.

You thought I must be spoken in darkness, but I am not a sin.

You thought I must be uttered with beauty, but I am not for show.

Does it surprise you to find me on a wide green lawn, laughing with a child?

Did you think I would avoid large crowds and school halls?

Have you found me in a solitary jog on a lonely road?

Did you know you can feel me even in mundane tasks? Mowing, weeding, building, planting, cleaning, driving?

Some people feel me even in weeping.

You decided I was so special that you must set rules around me like a cage. Rules would preserve my value, you reasoned. But do you know what happened instead? Through these rules, you grew to hate me.

Children now dread me.

Elders rehearse me.

Teens mock me.

I wish you could see that I'm more than what you've made me, see that I exist in poetry and perfection, as well as agony and intensity. You see, my home is in the deepest parts of your being. I exist wherever your soul resonates the strongest. In a silent, dark, moment, yes. But also in a raging rainstorm, a yardful of crickets, or a quickly scrawled letter. I can be as simple as one word, or no words at all.

I exist for you, my friend, yet you know me not.

I am prayer.

"Mom! Oh, no!"

Mom turned around in her seat and stared back at me. "What's wrong, Sarah?"

Five years old, I lifted my frantic face to her. "I lost my red doll. The one that squeaks. It's gone!"

Mom smiled. "Well, you had it when we left home, and we haven't stopped the car since then, so I'm sure it's in here somewhere."

"No," I argued, close to tears. "It's all the way gone!"

"It will show up, Sarah. Don't worry." She turned around and left me to my search.

Suddenly I remembered the solution. "Hey, Dad, stop the car! Let's pray!"

As a little girl, I was addicted to prayer. Everything had to be prayed over, from a lost red doll to a misplaced sock.

As I got older, however, my enthusiasm dimmed. Prayer lost its excitement.

I sat in prayer meeting with my parents, dreading the moment our pastor suggested, "Let's pray." We all eased to our knees and stayed there for what seemed like eternity. My only entertainment was to examine the pattern on the green carpet we knelt on.

I learned that prayer was a great time to giggle with my friends during Sabbath school. Nobody could get us in trouble! And later on I admitted that prayer had become decidedly boring.

"I can't concentrate while I'm praying," I confessed to Angie one day. "I usually end up thinking about everything I have to get done for the day instead."

"Me too," she agreed. "I wish there was something we could do to make prayer a little more exciting."

The answer came in the form of a guest speaker for one of my education classes. I knew the minute I saw Danny that he would have something interesting to tell us. A tall man in his early 30s, Danny served as a minister for a nearby church. He spent most of his time working as a spiritual mentor.

"One of the most important things I do with each new mentee," he told us that day, "is pray with them."

Before I could ask him, Danny answered my question. He folded his long frame into a classroom chair and smiled around the room at us. "I know most of you have been taught to close your eyes and fold your hands when you pray. And that's wonderful. I believe God deserves all the reverence we can give Him. But there are countless ways to pray besides the traditional ones."

"Like what?" A voice called from the back of the room.

"Let's see . . ." Danny's eyes sparkled as though he were discussing something that actually fascinated him. I leaned forward.

"One of my favorite ways to pray is to wander down by the river all by myself. I've memorized a lot of psalms, and I say them over to myself, giving them to God as prayers." Danny paused for a moment.

I gazed around the classroom and saw interest on every face.

"I like to pray as I jog. Having that time alone with God feels like a prayer to me. And sometimes I just sit and listen to praise music and pray like that. What do you think of those ideas?"

What did I think? I could hardly contain my enthusiasm! After class I approached Danny and thanked him for helping me realize that prayer had unlimited possibilities. For so long I'd been praying black-and-white prayers. Suddenly a whole new palette opened up to me.

If God is such a big God, shouldn't we have a big selection of ways to talk to Him? I believe He hears every prayer, from the popular "God help me!" to a wordless prayer of thanks from the top of a mountain.

With so many options, how could prayer ever be boring again? This God, the God I can talk to, is more accessible than I ever realized.

Reference Points:

"When you pray, do not be like the hypocrites, for they love to

pray standing in the synagogues and on the street corners to be seen by men. I tell you the truth, they have received their reward in full. But when you pray, go into your room, close the door and pray to your Father, who is unseen. Then your Father, who sees what is done in secret, will reward you. And when you pray, do not keep on babbling like pagans, for they think they will be heard because of their many words. Do not be like them, for your Father knows what you need before you ask him. This, then, is how you should pray: Our Father in heaven, hallowed be your name, your kingdom come, your will be done on earth as it is in heaven. Give us today our daily bread. Forgive us our debts, as we also have forgiven our debtors. And lead us not into temptation, but deliver us from the evil one" (Matthew 6:5-13).

"He will respond to the prayer of the destitute; he will not despise their plea" (Psalm 102:17).

"If you believe, you will receive whatever you ask for in prayer" (Matthew 21:22).

"Confess your sins to each other and pray for each other so that you may be healed. The prayer of a righteous man is powerful and effective" (James 5:16).

Chapter Fifteen

God *of the Learning*

"Are you coming or not?" Even over the phone Becca's voice sounds excited. I hear laughter and slamming doors in the background. "We're leaving right now if you want to come."

"Well—" I glance down the hall where Mom wrestles with our old Electrolux vacuum cleaner. She looks up and shrugs. Outside, the Friday afternoon sun sinks lower and lower over Duffy mountain. I bite my lip.

"I'd better not come," I finally decide. "I'm sorry. Have fun without me." I wonder if Becca knows what a tough decision I just made.

"OK, talk to you later." With a click, her voice disappears from the phone line and I slowly hang up the receiver.

"I'm not going," I repeat to myself as I sink into a kitchen chair and stare across the table at Charley. "I'm not going."

He looks up from a careful study of his bitten fingernails. "Did you want to go?"

I hit the table with an angry fist. "Of course I did! It's the Fourth of July. I want to do something fun." I try to swallow the persistent lump in my throat. "Would you have gone?"

Charley stretches out his long legs under the table and yawns. "Probably not," he replies simply.

"Why not? What's wrong with going out on Friday night?"

He sighs. "Sarah, there are just some things I don't do. Friday night is the beginning of Sabbath."

"But I can't support a belief I'm not convicted about!" I argue. "I don't know where I stand on the Sabbath yet. What am I supposed to do?" I bury my head in my hands and stare at the rough wood grain of the table.

"Well, that's up to you."

"I knew you would say that."

Down the hall the vacuum cleaner sputters to life. Mom whistles as she pulls it toward her bedroom.

"Well, I won't do anything just because Mom and Dad do it!" I explode. "I want to find my own beliefs!"

"So do I," Charley reminds me. He stares out the window at the disappearing sun. "I want to be independent too. But I've grown up Adventist. Keeping the Sabbath is a part of my life."

"Yeah. A part of my life that I don't understand," I grumble.

Charley glances up at me. "I don't want to change that part of my life, Sarah."

"So you stand up for it?" I glare. "Well, I can't do that. I'm not sure about the Sabbath yet, and I feel like a hypocrite when I defend it." Frustrated, I run a hand through my tousled hair. Most of my thoughts are a war between what I want and what my upbringing has taught me.

Charley leans forward, while his chair creaks in protest. "That's just it, Sarah. You don't *have* to feel convicted!"

I blink. "I don't?"

His blue eyes search mine. "Do Adventists have all the answers?"

I shrug. "Some people think we're supposed to."

"But we're human, too, right?"

"Yeah."

"Then what's wrong with admitting that we're still learning?" Charley persists.

"Nothing, I guess."

"Right!" He grins. "When I make a choice, I stick with the option that goes easiest on my conscience. Then I explain to people that I'm still figuring out what I believe."

I frown and lean forward on my elbows. "So you end up doing what Mom and Dad taught you anyway?"

"Usually."

"Even if you don't understand why?"

Charley nods. "Yeah. It gives me an obligation to find out why they taught me that way, and then to decide if I agree."

I flick a bread crumb to the floor and ponder my brother's words. "That makes sense. You respect Mom and Dad so much that you're willing to trust their judgment until you know the answers for yourself."

"That's right." Charley pushes back his chair and stands up. "I've got to help Dad clean the shop before Sabbath. See you later."

As the screen door squeaks shut behind him, I review our conversation. Why hadn't I thought of that approach before? Instead of agonizing over the war in my mind between my upbringing and my friends, I realize that I've found an easier solution.

Almost invariably, choices that differ from what I've been taught result in pricks from my conscience. *Why does this bother me so much?* I wonder in frustration. *I'm old enough to make my own choices.* But the voice in my head reminds me that I've violated something I've learned was wrong. Usually I end up feeling just as miserable as if I had made the "right" choice and missed the fun anyway.

Miserable. I sigh and glance around the kitchen. *Here I am, sitting at home on a Friday night, while my friends all are having a great time without me. Of course I'm miserable.* I absently kick my right foot and bang it against a table leg.

What am I supposed to do? Rubbing my sore toe, I glance at our hen-shaped cookie jar. *Well, I definitely don't want to take after you, chicken.* The jar sits placidly on our kitchen counter, its enamel feathers unruffled by my insult.

Tell the truth.

The thought strikes me as strongly as though Charley had not just proposed it two minutes earlier. Suddenly my life seems simpler than it has been in months. Instead of beating around the burning bush when faced with a tricky decision, I realize that I should tell the plain and simple truth.

But what will you say?

I grin ruefully. The voices in my head have not disappeared, but I have a reply for them this time.

I am a Christian. I am Adventist. That does not make me perfect. I am still learning what I believe. But I've grown up hearing that I should not do that. So because I trust my parents' judgment, I am going to avoid doing that until I know for myself whether it's right or wrong.

Satisfied, I lean back in my chair.

What if they ask why? The voice returns.

Then I'll tell them the truth, I retort hotly. *I will tell them that I serve a God whom I want to please more than anything in the world. A God who wants me to find the answers on my own. A God, my God, of the learning.*

For the first time in months the voice in my head cannot reply. I smile at the cookie jar. *Guess you're on your own now, little chicken.*

Standing up, I peer down the hall to where the vacuum cleaner has just wheezed to a stop. "Mom? Hey, could you use some help before sundown comes?"

Reference Points:

"I will instruct you and teach you in the way you should go; I will counsel you and watch over you" (Psalm 32:8).

"Whatever is true, whatever is noble, whatever is right, whatever is pure, whatever is lovely, whatever is admirable—if anything is excellent or praiseworthy—think about such things. Whatever you have learned or received or heard from me, or seen in me—put it into practice. And the God of peace will be with you" (Philippians 4:8, 9).

"The unfolding of your words gives light; it gives understanding to the simple" (Psalm 119:130).

"If any of you lacks wisdom, he should ask God, who gives generously to all without finding fault, and it will be given to him" (James 1:5).

Chapter Sixteen

God *of Action*

I still wonder what happened to that hobo. Dad picked him up on the road one day, promising a shower and some home-cooked food.

"You're welcome here," Mom told him that night at supper. "You can stay a few days if you need to."

He thanked her and took another bite of his spaghetti. (He was always very conscientious about saying thank you.)

And he stayed.

It must have been at least two weeks. He hung around the house during the day. In the evening he sat on the porch with my parents and talked about grown-up subjects while they watched the hummingbirds fight over the red feeder.

One night after supper we pulled him toward the woods and showed him the red-ripe clusters of chokecherries. "They're great to throw at people," we hinted shyly.

And suddenly he became a kid again. Stripping a handful of berries right off the vine, he pelted us with a volley of ammunition that sent us dodging for cover. We schemed and planned and attacked him from three sides with our own handfuls of berries. Soon the four of us sported broad purple splotches, and the bushes were bare once again.

We watched him with wonder after that, idolizing this beloved stranger with holes in his jeans.

"Can he stay forever?" I asked Mom as she ironed in the kitchen.

"No," she responded firmly. "He needs to move on."

And after several more days he did just that. I think he sensed my parents' nervousness. You can't let a hobo get too close to your family, after all. It isn't safe. I'm sure there were a million other reasons he had to go, but I didn't approve of any of them.

We sent him off well: a backpack full of food, freshly washed laundry, and a complimentary Bible. I think I cried when he left.

He phoned us several times from various places around the country. Every call was collect. And after a while my parents began to refuse the calls. By then I was old enough to understand that they had to. But I still wondered about him, especially when I passed a certain scraggly chokecherry bush.

I'm older now. The memory of that hobo has faded until I can barely recall his smile-wrinkled face. But I hold tightly to the essence of those two weeks. Why? I don't exactly know. Maybe because during that short space of time I grew to respect my parents more than ever before. Although I was young, I knew it cost a lot to house a hobo. I knew they were worried about letting him play with us. And I sensed, after the first week, their uneasiness at his prolonged stay in our backyard.

I saw their hospitality as somehow noble. I remembered the verse in the Bible in which Jesus speaks to the people at His second coming:

"Then the King will say to those on His right, 'Come, you who are blessed by my Father; take your inheritance, the kingdom prepared for you since the creation of the world. For I was hungry and you gave me something to eat, I was thirsty and you gave me something to drink, I was a stranger and you invited me in, I needed clothes and you clothed me, I was sick and you looked after me, I was in prison and you came to visit me.'

"Then the righteous will answer him, 'Lord, when did we see you hungry and feed you, or thirsty and give you something to drink? When did we see you a stranger and invite you in, or needing clothes and clothe you? When did we see you sick or in prison and go to visit you?'

"The King will reply, 'I tell you the truth, whatever you did for one of the least of these brothers of mine, you did for me'" (Matthew 25:34-40).

In my 10-year-old mind I wondered, *Would I have the courage to do that when I grow up? Could I be that brave?*

Now, 10 years later, I still wonder. People don't trust anyone to stay in their house unless they're good friends. And besides, it's not very smart to keep a hobo in your dorm room. So my options may be limited.

Even if I don't house a hobo, though, there are thousands of other ways to reach "the least of these." In the past I viewed service as something glorious. But now I know that true service is often met with ingratitude. I know that many times the person you serve doesn't realize you're helping them. And I know too that the least of these includes more than friendly hoboes. It includes those I wish to ignore: the strange, the unfriendly, the misfits that everyone avoids. To be a true servant I must lay pride and inhibition aside in the act of reaching out to God's children. And it won't always be as fun as a chokecherry fight in the summer.

Would I have the courage? Could I be that brave?

My parents' experience is only one of countless examples I want to follow. Examples of a selfless life of service. Examples of individuals wholly committed to their God, the God of action.

Reference Points:

"Dear children, let us not love with words or tongue but with actions and in truth" (1 John 3:18).

"Jesus did many other things as well. If every one of them were written down, I suppose that even the whole world would not have room for the books that would be written" (John 21:25).

"Faith by itself, if it is not accompanied by action, is dead" (James 2:17).

"They claim to know God, but by their actions they deny him. They are detestable, disobedient and unfit for doing anything good" (Titus 1:16).

"By their fruit you will recognize them" (Matthew 7:16).

"When you give to the needy, do not let your left hand know what your right hand is doing, so that your giving may be in secret. Then your Father, who sees what is done in secret, will reward you" (Matthew 6:3, 4).

"Jesus looked at him and loved him. 'One thing you lack,' he said. 'Go, sell everything you have and give to the poor, and you will have treasure in heaven. Then come, follow me'" (Mark 10:21).

Chapter Seventeen

God *Who Is Human*

(Based on Mark 9:33, 34; 5:24-30)

It was one of the worst days of My life.

You know the kind—hot, sweat-sticky, with air hanging thick over you like a suffocating scarf. Of all the kinds of days, these are the worst.

It started out all right. I woke up before anyone else and fixed Myself some breakfast. Then, as I prepared some food for them, My friends stirred to life.

Instead of shouting, "Good morning, Master," as usual, they immediately began to quarrel. There's nothing too earth-shattering about that, but today they picked something annoying to fight about—Me.

"I'm going to be the greatest," Peter mumbled, singsong-like, to his brother, Andrew. Andrew, of course "accidentally," kicked dust all over Peter's sandals. Well, that started a scuffle, and pretty soon Judas and Thomas got involved.

And do you know what? By the time I had breakfast ready for them, those men were filthy, angry, and pouting like a bunch of babies. I almost laughed at them, but I took a bite of fish instead.

Like I said, this was one of the worst days of My life.

We got on the road later than I expected. As usual, that was hard for Me to take. It reminded Me of living at home again—I'd always be ready for synagogue earlier than My older brothers, and they would scurry around and glower at Me for being so punctual.

Anyhow, we finally packed our belongings and set off for Jerusalem. The fighting didn't stop. In fact, the farther we hiked, the worse it became, until I felt as though I would go crazy if I didn't say something.

"He likes me better than you," James whispered to Thomas.

"Huh. I doubt it," Thomas scoffed, scuffing a rock along the road. "You never say anything witty or offer to find Him a drink. I, on the other hand, make it a priority to be courteous and respectful."

"I suppose you think that assures you the highest rank in His kingdom, don't you?"

"I know it, pal." Thomas accidentally scuffed his rock into My sandal, where it firmly lodged for safety.

"I'm sorry, Master," he sniveled as I bent to pick it out. "Will You forgive me?"

No! I wanted to shout in his face. *No, I will not forgive you!* But at the last minute I looked to the sky and remembered My Father. By the time I turned to him I was smiling and had remembered a million reasons why I loved him.

This battle continued all through the dusty afternoon. As the sun lowered toward the scrub-brush horizon, I spotted the crowd. They'd been waiting outside the city all day, no doubt. I knew I loved them with all My heart, but something made My steps falter as I drew near.

"Jesus! Jesus!" They reached and clawed for Me like wild beasts. Peter and the others did their best to fend them off. John managed "Excuse me, please" every few minutes, but nothing could stop their frenzy.

"Save my boy! He will die!"

"Do You love me? Heal my arm!"

"My father is a leper!"

The calls went on and on. Before I realized it, I stood inside the eye of the storm, amid a swirling, stinking mass of helpless people. If I had sunk to My knees and prayed for strength as My impulse directed, I would have been trampled under a mob of feet. It struck me as ironic, and again I nearly laughed in their faces, but I realized their truly hopeless state and restrained Myself.

One man, an old fellow with large moles and a scraggly beard, kept yanking on the corner of My robe. Several impatient children shouted My name in headache-forming voices. Mothers thrust their babies at Me with the vehemence a meat-seller reserves for marketing his wares. I believe they would have dropped them at My feet if they knew I would bless them anyway.

I could not breathe. The stench of so many bodies, close-packed for hours and finally stirring the air, nauseated Me. Several times I felt My hands rise as though to push them out of My way, so I clenched My fists against My sides instead.

Father, help Me! I pleaded as a large man stepped squarely on both sets of toes. *Help Me keep My sanity and My love for these people. Remind Me of why I came here.*

My prayer seemed nearly useless. I had to do something to stop this nightmare. Knowing I might yell some of the words I'd often heard Peter employ if I didn't act soon, I put up a hand to silence the crowd. Behind Me a slight rustle caught My attention, and I felt a little energy leave My body.

"Who touched Me?" I demanded loudly.

Amid the guffaws of the pressing mob, I had to smile too. I knew already that it was the woman behind Me, the one who hid her face each time I looked her way. I knew she longed for a healing. But thanks to My Father's incredible timing, she got her health and I got My reminder, all at once. Suddenly, in that tiny instant, I remembered why I had come down.

Not for the miracles, though they were rewarding.

Not for the love, though when it came, it filled My soul.

I came for the trials, the hurt, the pain, and the anger. I came for the temptation to yell at immature friends. The option to turn my back on helpless individuals. The opportunity to swear, to shout, to degrade, and to scoff at My fellow human beings. I came to experience all this without sin—a job far harder than I could ever explain. *Oh,* I thought grimly as I rubbed My aching toes, *I do hope they realize exactly how thoroughly I have been tempted for them.*

"Jesus! Jesus, over here! My niece is a paralytic. Can You—"

I smiled, holding peace in My heart once again.

Yes, I can.

Reference Points:

"For this reason he had to be made like his brothers in every way, in order that he might become a merciful and faithful high priest in service to God, and that he might make atonement for the sins of the people. Because he himself suffered when he was tempted, he is able to help those who are being tempted" (Hebrews 2:17, 18).

"No temptation has seized you except what is common to man. And God is faithful; he will not let you be tempted beyond what you can bear. But when you are tempted, he will also provide a way out so that you can stand up under it" (1 Corinthians 10:13).

"We do not have a high priest who is unable to sympathize with our weaknesses, but we have one who has been tempted in every way, just as we are—yet was without sin. Let us then approach the throne of grace with confidence, so that we may receive mercy and find grace to help us in our time of need" (Hebrews 4:15, 16).

"Your attitude should be the same as that of Christ Jesus: Who, being in very nature God, did not consider equality with God something to be grasped, but made himself nothing, taking the very nature of a servant, being made in human likeness. And being found in appearance as a man, he humbled himself and became obedient to death—even death on a cross!" (Philippians 2:5-8).

"Direct my footsteps according to your word; let no sin rule over me" (Psalm 119:133).

Chapter Eighteen

God Who Values

(Based on Luke 19:1-10)

I've always been an outcast. Maybe it's because I've always had an independent personality. In fact, I've been totally independent for most of my life. Ever since children began teasing me because I was short, I have not cared deeply about any human being.

"Here comes little Zacchaeus!" they would shout. "Look how big his younger sister is! Why don't you catch up to her, little Zacchaeus?"

I ached to grow. Each night I stretched as tall as I could in the hopes that overnight my body would lengthen just a little bit more.

But it never happened.

Finally I got tired of their comments and lashed back at them instead of laughing. "Short, yourself. At least I don't have a nose as long as a Torah scroll! Leave me alone!"

At first my friends had taken it in fun. But eventually they pulled away and left me alone with my anger. I was finally safe from hurt—and from love. But somewhere, deep inside, I still wanted to impress them, wanted to show them that I, little Zacchaeus, was big enough to deserve respect after all. My only avenue was money, and in a blind moment of self-torture I chose to be a tax collector.

To this day I'm not sure why I consented to work for those Romans. True, I received a hefty salary, but my new status as "rich man" didn't affect my compatriots' attitude in the slightest.

"Taken to cheating, have you?" they hissed when I collected their money. "You're a traitor, little Zacchaeus. Nothing but a dirty traitor. And I despise you!"

I pretended not to care. But inside I shriveled a little more each time someone scowled at me or called me a name. I wasn't worth anything, after all. Little Zacchaeus had turned out bad, just as my classmates had always predicted. I had no hope for acceptance among my people now, but something drove me on. If I could only become a little richer . . .

Higher, higher, I charged their taxes. Lower, lower, sank their respect. Nobody spoke to me except the girl who cleaned my mansion. But in her eyes I read the same scorn that the housewives and rabbis, carpenters and fishermen directed at me. I hated my life. I was a dishonest fool, and I knew it. But still I kept up my pursuit of money.

One day as I sat in the wet heat of my booth, I heard a wisp of conversation that intrigued me.

"Have you met Him?" asked one.

"Not yet," responded the other. "But He comes to our village soon. Oh, only to touch His robes, the robes of this Man who loves even Romans . . ."

"They say He forgives sins."

"We shall see," the other replied. "We shall see."

"Who? Who is this Man?" I leaned from my booth and strained toward those voices. My robe stretched tightly against my chest, and I felt as though I were choking. But the speakers were gone—or merely ignoring me, as the rest of my people did. I sank back down on my padded bench and pondered the gold ring on my right thumb. I would give all my rings to talk with a Man who could forgive my sins.

And sooner than I expected, my chance came along.

I was in a crowd that day, a hot, sticky crowd moving hurriedly along the streets. As usual, nobody talked to me. But I caught an excitement in the air that prompted me to talk to a young man standing beside me.

"Where are they rushing to?" I asked offhandedly.

He turned a sunburned face toward me. "Jesus," he responded. "Jesus of Nazareth passes this way soon. Ahead." He motioned with a callused finger, and I strained to see. Too many heads, too many bodies stood in my way. Jesus of Nazareth? He was the Man the voices had spoken of. The Man who loved even Romans.

Before I could think, I found myself scrambling up the nearest tree. It was rough and had thorns—sycamore, I think it was—but I didn't even notice the rips it tore in my expensive robe. I didn't hear the laughter from the crowd as I balanced on a thick branch. I only knew I must see this Man and talk with Him about my sins.

I couldn't help thinking, as I sat there and scanned the tightly packed crowd, that this tree represented my whole life. Constantly I'd climbed higher and higher in an effort to reach a level the people would respect. But instead I'd ended up as distanced from them as I was now, perched like a fool in this uncomfortable tree.

I watched their heads like a bird of prey, searching for this Jesus, Man of Nazareth. For once I didn't wonder who had paid their taxes and who had slipped by unnoticed. Instead I searched each turban-covered head for a sign of the one who forgave sins.

The roar of the crowd heightened, and I had the sensation of an approaching windstorm. From my position I couldn't understand what the masses shouted, and I wondered if He had already passed me by.

Suddenly a voice rang out above the rest. "Zacchaeus!"

I peered downward.

"Zacchaeus, get down from that tree!"

A friendly plain face stared up at me from the other side of the street. I'd never met Him before. Yet the crowd fell silent at His words. He must be important. Could this be—

"Zacchaeus, may I have the honor of dining with you tonight? I would like that very much. Zacchaeus, come down from there. I'm coming to your house today!"

He laughed up at me, but it wasn't a snicker of dislike. It was rich and full of joy, as though He and I shared some wonderful secret. As though He and I were equals!

Eager to talk with this Man Jesus, I scrambled down from the tree and followed the crowd that pressed tightly about Him. Eventually we stopped and He began to speak—low, melodious, and stirring. He told stories of rich men and poor men, sadness and joy. And as I stood there in that sweaty crowd of people, I began to feel a new sensation. When He glanced around at our faces, His expression did not change to fury on seeing mine. Instead He looked at all of us with the same radiant love. He knew who I was. He had called me by name. And yet He did not mock me or turn His face away in disgust.

He had, in fact, stopped an entire crowd to call me down from my tree. He had asked to join me for dinner, as though we were friends already! He had treated me as an equal!

I stood there, silent, in the crowd and smiled at Him. I smiled for the first time in many years at this Jesus, this Man who had already forgiven the sins I loathed. Who loved me through my prickles and anger and in spite of my faults. Who valued me for exactly who I was.

Suddenly I didn't seem quite so terrible to myself. If this incredible Man valued me, maybe others could too.

Reference Points:

"If anyone is in Christ, he is a new creation; the old has gone, the new has come!" (2 Corinthians 5:17).

"Jesus entered Jericho and was passing through. A man was there by the name of Zacchaeus; he was a chief tax collector and was wealthy. He wanted to see who Jesus was, but being a short man he could not, because of the crowd. So he ran ahead and climbed a sycamore-fig tree to see him, since Jesus was coming that way. When Jesus reached the spot, he looked up and said to him, 'Zacchaeus, come down immediately. I must stay at your house today.' So he came down at once and welcomed him gladly. All the people saw this and began to mutter, 'He has gone to be the guest of a "sinner."' But Zacchaeus stood up and said to the Lord, 'Look, Lord! Here and now I give half of my possessions to the poor, and if I have cheated anybody out of anything, I will pay back four times the amount.' Jesus said to him, 'Today salvation has come to this house, because this

man, too, is a son of Abraham. For the Son of Man came to seek and to save what was lost' " (Luke 19:1-10).

"You are a chosen people, a royal priesthood, a holy nation, a people belonging to God, that you may declare the praises of him who called you out of darkness into his wonderful light" (1 Peter 2:9).

"I urge you, brothers, in view of God's mercy, to offer your bodies as living sacrifices, holy and pleasing to God—this is your spiritual act of worship. Do not conform any longer to the pattern of this world, but be transformed by the renewing of your mind. Then you will be able to test and approve what God's will is—his good, pleasing and perfect will" (Romans 12:1, 2).

Chapter Nineteen

God *of Wonders*

The year is 1977. In a tiny gray house by the stream, a young woman and her husband prepare for bed. But she doesn't feel like sleeping.

"I must have eaten something bad this evening," she complains. "My stomach feels terrible." She crawls out of bed and pads to the bathroom for a warm shower. And suddenly, standing beneath the warm jets of water, she knows. "It's time!"

Minutes later the couple race to the hospital in their tiny tan car. By the next morning Karen has given birth to a healthy baby girl.

Or has she?

"What's wrong?" she asks the doctor, who still hasn't returned her baby. "Where is she?"

He looks at her over his glasses. "There seems to be a bit of a problem."

The couple learn that their daughter has congenital microopthalmia, or "small eye from birth." Sarah's left eye never completely formed and lay sightless in its socket. Her right eye retained a cord connecting the lens to the retina that should have dissolved months ago. As Sarah grew, this cord would remain the same size and eventually pull the growing eye apart, causing blindness in her right eye as well. Surgery was imperative to save her sight.

"It's a simple operation," the doctor assures them. "Sarah will be just fine. The only drawback is that we must cut through her right lens to reach the cord. She will wear high-magnification contacts or glasses for the rest of her life."

"Anything," they agree eagerly. "Anything to let her see."

Carefully the doctor makes the first incision, removes the lens and cord, and sews the eye together again. Carefully the couple care for their daughter until the day the bandages can be removed. She is well again!

Or is she?

Several weeks later they take her back for a checkup. "She's stone blind," a stoic doctor informs them after a few quick tests. "Can't see a thing."

They sit, stunned, in his office. How could a simple operation go so awry? The surgeons offer no explanations—and no hope. Discouraged, the couple prepare for life with a blind daughter. Self-blaming questions rage through their minds, but nothing softens the truth: in the room next to theirs a small blind girl awakes to even the softest whisper. She turns her head toward noise instead of light. She stares vacantly at ceilings and walls. She is irreversibly blind.

Or is she?

"I'd like to have a special service for Sarah," the couple's pastor tells them one day. "I'd like to anoint her head with oil and pray for her with some elders from the church. Would that be all right with you?"

The couple look at each other doubtfully. What more can go wrong? Can they endure the blinding hope—and then the aching disappointment—of God's will? Should they subject themselves to this torture?

"When can you come over?" Rollie asks softly.

Several nights later a small group of elders gathers in Rollie and Karen's living room. Reverently they bow their heads over the small girl inside their circle, beseeching God for a miraculous healing.

Periodically someone waves a hand in front of Sarah's face. No response. After several hours of prayer and silence, they finally stand to leave. Quietly they file from the house. At least *their* children can see.

Weeks pass. One winter day Karen walks across the living room. Stealing a quick glance at the crib, she sees Sarah's open eyes follow her movements.

She must be imagining.

Soft as a cat she repeats the motion, and just as silently the baby's fully formed eye follows her progress.

"Rollie, come here!"

They repeat the procedure several times, each time convinced it must be coincidental, and finally resort to a silent brightly colored rattle.

"You do it," Karen instructs her mother, who is visiting at the time.

With shaking hands Grandma holds the toy out to her granddaughter. Sarah reaches eagerly for the noiseless offering, unaware of the miracle she has just revealed.

"She can see!" Almost afraid to say the words, Sarah's family repeats the phrase over and over. "Sarah can see!"

A trip to the doctor's office confirms the fact. Sarah's good eye has been healed. Once again the doctors have no explanation. But Sarah's family knows: God's will had, after all, been sight.

Now, 19 years later, my family still loves to tell me this story. And I, of course, love to hear it. Although I can't remember the moment of my healing or, for that matter, the months of my blindness, I'm still amazed at the silent transformation that God performed inside my right eye.

I see today. I wear a prosthesis in my left eye and strong contacts in my right. But I see. I have my driver's license, and I play sports. I can see falling stars and flying birds. I don't know why God chose to give me vision, and I don't know how long I'll keep it. But I'm content with the knowledge that His plan includes these years of light and color, shape and shadow.

Why do I tell this story? Do I want you to marvel at God's working in my life alone? Do I want to humble those who have no miracles to relate? Or do I simply like to see printed words on a smooth page that highlight my experiences?

I tell this story because I believe there are countless stories like it across the world. I believe even those who feel void of sensational experiences possess some incredible evidence of God's presence in their lives. I believe even those who do not know God, who do not want to know Him, have in their past or future some tangible reminder of God's direction.

You see, I believe that even if I had not been rescued from a sightless existence, God's plan for me would have been just as incredible. If I had never gone blind, I would still sense His presence in me. His plan includes far more miracles than you or I will ever comprehend.

I tell my story simply to remind you of God's power. I want you to know Him, my God, this God of mystery and miracles, whose power and love stretches far beyond infinity and into the future. The God of wonders.

Reference Points:

"I will lead the blind by ways they have not known, along unfamiliar paths I will guide them; I will turn the darkness into light before them and make the rough places smooth. These are the things I will do; I will not forsake them" (Isaiah 42:16).

"One thing I do know. I was blind but now I see!" (John 9:25).

"Come and see what God has done, how awesome his works in man's behalf!" (Psalm 66:5).

"See, the former things have taken place, and new things I declare; before they spring into being I announce them to you" (Isaiah 42:9).

"You created my inmost being; you knit me together in my mother's womb. I praise you because I am fearfully and wonderfully made; your works are wonderful, I know that full well. My frame was not hidden from you when I was made in the secret place. When I was woven together in the depths of the earth, your eyes saw my unformed body. All the days ordained for me were written in your book before one of them came to be. How precious to me are your thoughts, O God! How vast is the sum of them! Were I to count them, they would outnumber the grains of sand. When I awake, I am still with you" (Psalm 139:13-18).

Chapter Twenty

God *the Believable*

A seagull calls and whirls deep in the sky. Below it a sandy road stretches long toward the horizon. As the bird flies northward, it passes over two men deep in discussion. One, the one with reddish tints in his hair and sun freckles across his forearms, seems to be persuading the other.

"Thomas," he speaks urgently. "What more does it take? Don't you believe me yet? I'm a doctor. I deal with science, and science is facts."

The tall deep-eyed youth shakes his head. "No. No, it will take more than your word to convince me, Luke. I am not a doctor, and I may be young, but I have often been wrong." He pauses to stare up at the gliding gull. "And my many mistakes have taught me something more valuable than any medical profession."

"And what is that?" Luke's voice carries the slightest hint of amusement.

Thomas catches his tone. "You laugh now, but I tell you, I'm not a fool. My mistakes have taught me to wait. Wait and watch." He motions to a curve in the trail ahead. "If you told me the road ended in a cliff around that bend, I would not turn and travel another way."

"What would you do, Thomas?"

"I would, of course, walk to the 'end of the road' to see for myself. If a traveler asked me later about the same road, I could offer firsthand knowledge instead of relaying the possibly wrong opinion of another." He scuffs over a rock with his sandal. "Do you see what I mean?"

Luke scratches a freckled forearm. "Thomas, you should have been a scholar. You have a mind that would take you far in the world of learning."

"Thank you."

"But that does not mean I agree with your philosophy. I too once held the very same belief. But when I met the Master—"

"I know, I know," Thomas sighs. "When you met the Master all doubts disappeared. Luke, my doubts disappeared too. I know He does—*did*—inexplicable things. But I can't change my personality just because—"

"Because 10 of your closest friends say they saw the risen Master?"

He sighs again. "Yes."

Luke watches as a cloud's edges gild against the darkening sky. "Then I will not try to convince you. But I will not relinquish my belief, either. I know I saw Jesus, alive and breathing, in the upper room that night. I only wish you had seen Him too."

"So do I," Thomas responds heartily. "But until I feel that gash in His side—until I trace the nailprints with my own fingers—I cannot fully accept this story. I am sorry."

"So am I."

They walk along in silence. Finally the two arrive at the city and hurry through its streets to the old familiar house where the others wait. Thomas wonders at the sudden energy that charges the men so recently plagued with sorrow.

"It is the Master's presence," they tell him. "We know He lives."

Thomas nods curtly and settles down in his usual corner. Then, as Peter and Thaddaeus joke about the many Pharisees who would pay dearly for a key to this room, a strange thing happens. Where once there had been nothing but wood and dust, a Man in blazing white now stands.

Thomas jumps to his feet and points at the Man, who smiles unmistakably like their Master. Peter lets out an "Aha!" of surprise, and Luke watches Thomas.

The Man opens His arms, palms upward, in a familiar gesture of friendship. He speaks softly to the now-silent gathering. "Peace be with you."

"And with You, Master," Peter answers warmly, impulsively.

But the Master's eyes turn toward Thomas. He beckons with a nail-scarred hand. "Come here, Thomas."

Thomas shakes his head. "I see; I see," he whispers.

"But I want you to feel, Thomas," Jesus laughs softly.

Silently, slowly, Thomas walks toward his Lord.

"Give Me your hand, Thomas."

Those facing Jesus vowed later that a tear had coursed down His cheek. "Give Me your hand."

Thomas obeys, his fingers trembling, his eyes downcast. Deftly Jesus takes the hand and moves it along His left wrist and over a round jagged scar in the skin. The same gesture is repeated on the right wrist.

A great sob wracks Thomas's frame. "I see, Master; I see."

"Wait."

Again, Jesus takes the trembling hand. This time He places it over His side and presses the fingers deep into an angry red scar in the flesh.

Thomas jerks back as though the wound were poisonous. Has he caused this pain? Through a haze of unshed tears, he holds his Master's gaze. "My Lord!" He chokes on the words. "My Lord and my God."

Jesus releases his hand and takes a step backward. Thomas retreats to his seat in the corner, sobs convulsing his thin shoulders. This Man before him is indeed the Master. The same Master who had walked those fly-ridden roads with him for years. The same Master who had suffered alone on a cross just days before, forsaken by all His friends. The same Master who smiles on Him now, a strange peace filling His eyes. "What do you think now, Thomas?"

Several days later Luke again walks the stone-strewn path with his friend.

Thomas turns toward the doctor. "I got my wish, did I not?"

Luke throws back his head and laughs up at the sky. "Indeed you did! You saw with your own eyes!"

"But I got more than that," Thomas continues. "I gained the

knowledge that here or in heaven, in life or in death, this God of ours is a God to believe. When He said He would rise, He meant exactly that. I learned that I must take Him at His word, and much more often. And because I believe, I can do just that."

The two friends smile at each other. Behind them a seagull dips over the horizon and disappears from view.

Reference Points:

"I tell you the truth, if you have faith as small as a mustard seed, you can say to this mountain, 'Move from here to there' and it will move. Nothing will be impossible for you" (Matthew 17:20).

"Now Thomas (called Didymus), one of the Twelve, was not with the disciples when Jesus came. So the other disciples told him, 'We have seen the Lord!' But he said to them, 'Unless I see the nail marks in his hands and put my finger where the nails were, and put my hand into his side, I will not believe it.' A week later his disciples were in the house again, and Thomas was with them. Though the doors were locked, Jesus came and stood among them and said, 'Peace be with you!' Then he said to Thomas, 'Put your finger here; see my hands. Reach out your hand and put it into my side. Stop doubting and believe.' Thomas said to him, 'My Lord and my God!' Then Jesus told him, 'Because you have seen me, you have believed; blessed are those who have not seen and yet have believed.' Jesus did many other miraculous signs in the presence of his disciples, which are not recorded in this book. But these are written that you may believe that Jesus is the Christ, the Son of God, and that by believing you may have life in his name" (John 20:24-31).

"Immediately the boy's father exclaimed, 'I do believe; help me overcome my unbelief!'" (Mark 9:24).

"Jesus replied, 'I tell you the truth, if you have faith and do not doubt, not only can you do what was done to the fig tree, but also you can say to this mountain, "Go, throw yourself into the sea," and it will be done'" (Matthew 21:21).

Chapter Twenty-one

God *the Capable*

What do I need for work on Grounds today? Eager to feel the dirt between my fingers, I survey our tool supply speculatively. Finally I settle on a pair of gardening gloves, a rake, a trowel, and a five-gallon bucket. Placing them in a cart, I wheel the whole collection outdoors.

Perfect! The sky, clear except for a few lacy clouds, arches over my head like a tightly stretched blue tent. A cacophony of birdsong demands my attention. And the grass, like the weeds I plan to tackle today, greens and grows almost visibly.

I wave to the driver of a departing cement truck as I round the corner of the Grounds building. "I wonder why he was here?" I ask myself absently.

At the edge of the building, I pull the cart to a stop. Oh, great. A large green tractor implement sits squarely in my way through a small gate. "Well, I'll just move it," I decide. Rolling up my sleeves, I squat in front of the implement and pull. After several minutes of exertion, I inch it far enough away to allow me through.

"Finally!" I mutter. "Now let's move!" Grabbing the silver handle of my cart, I back quickly through the gate.

Something feels funny.

I take another step.

Yes, something is definitely wrong.

In another step, I realize the problem. With a screech loud enough to bring all the fire trucks in College Place, I leap backward and land on the solid sidewalk again. "Wet cement!"

I gasp in horror as I stare at the deep footprints I have just left in the thick slab of drying cement. Too embarrassed to blush, I quickly scan the campus. If no one has seen, I can sneak away and leave my footprints to remind the world of an anonymous klutz.

My gaze sweeps over a lone figure at the end of the sidewalk, then back again. *Warren!* "Did you see what just happened?" I ask, willing my voice to stop shaking.

He chuckles. "Not in time to stop it." His laughter grows, and I peer around me, hoping nobody else can hear.

"Shhh!" I warn, then cover my face with my hands. "What should I do? Gene will *kill* me when he sees this mess . . . Hey, why aren't you at work?"

Still chuckling, Warren heads toward the site of my accident. "My boss just called me up to say I should put 'caution' tape around the wet cement."

It's just too much. I sink to my knees by the mutilated slab. The footprints, marching backward in cavernous determination, cannot be ignored. "You've got to help me," I plead, "or your boss will fire us both!"

"Maybe we could use some of this extra stuff to level it off," he suggests, pointing at what looks like a large pile of chunky gray peanut butter.

"But it's so . . . *big*. Shouldn't concrete be smooth?"

"Do you want to leave the slab like this?"

Humbled, I scoop a handful of the gravel into my first footprint and try to pat it down. It looks, well, lumpy, and I wail in despair. Warren only laughs.

Just as I reach for another handful of the offending cement, a familiar voice stops me cold.

"What's this?" Gene asks from somewhere above my head. "Who walked in my fresh cement?"

Under the gaze of the only witness to my crime, my conscience bears down. "Uh, well, I sort of . . . did," I mumble.

"What?"

"I did," I admit, wishing I could bury myself in the concrete I hate. "I didn't know it was— I accidentally walked into— Well, see, I've been trying to fix it!"

"You're doing it all wrong!" Gene squats beside me and scrapes the excess gravel from my drying footprints. "Bring me a hose and a broom. Are there any old boards around here?"

When I return, I can't even recognize the site of my folly. Covered over with concrete again, the footprints have nearly disappeared.

"I'm so, so, sorry," I begin. "I don't know how I could have—"

"Hey, don't worry about it!" Gene smiles and wipes his crusty hands on his jeans. "I'm just glad I showed up right then!"

I nod gratefully and reach for my garden cart again. *This time,* I think ruefully, *I'll wheel it* around *the gate.*

My life is dotted with embarrassing experiences that somehow resurface at large social gatherings. *"Do you remember the time you learned how to drive a stick shift?" "What about the day you drove a tractor across the front campus lawn?" "Remember when you nearly cut my ear off, trimming my hair?"* As hard as I try, I can't erase these mistakes.

The Concrete Incident, however, exists as a welcome exception. Gene solved my problem that day. Swiftly, capably, without a grudge, he filled in the footprints that gave me away and turned my shame into relief.

Someone else saves my day more often than I admit.

Jesus does everything in His power to keep me from making unnecessary mistakes. But like the tractor implement placed in front of the slab, I take it upon myself to remove any precautionary obstacles. I insist on traveling *my* direction instead of heeding the context clues that point me somewhere else. And not until I've already left my footprints do I realize that Jesus might have been right to begin with.

This moment would be a prime time to ask for assistance. But I'm more concerned about hiding my mistake from my peers. I sink to my knees and quickly try to cover the mess I've made. *I can han-*

dle it myself, I mutter. *I got myself in this mess, and I'll get myself out.*

But I succeed only in making my problems worse. Just as I'm ready to give up, Jesus steps in and swiftly, capably, without a grudge, erases the evidence of my folly.

I remain on my knees. Once more I'm awed at His problem-solving expertise: *I'm just glad I got here on time. . . .*

On time? Maybe next time I'll ask Him a little sooner. Maybe next time I'll realize that I don't have the power to right every wrong. Maybe next time I'll turn immediately and ask my God, the God who is capable, if He will handle my dilemmas.

Reference Points:

"To him who is able to keep you from falling and to present you before his glorious presence without fault and with great joy—to the only God our Savior be glory, majesty, power and authority, through Jesus Christ our Lord, before all ages, now and forevermore! Amen" (Jude 1:24, 25).

"A righteous man may have many troubles, but the Lord delivers him from them all" (Psalm 34:19).

"Jesus replied, 'What is impossible with men is possible with God'" (Luke 18:27).

"The Israelites said to the Lord, 'We have sinned. Do with us whatever you think best, but please rescue us now'" (Judges 10:15).

"'Because he loves me,' says the Lord, 'I will rescue him; I will protect him, for he acknowledges my name. He will call upon me, and I will answer him; I will be with him in trouble, I will deliver him and honor him. With long life will I satisfy him and show him my salvation'" (Psalm 91:14-16).

Chapter Twenty-two

God *Who Heals*

(Based on Mark 10:46-52)

I know this spot well.

Each morning I scrabble my way from my father's home to this hard-packed spot by the road. It's always the same.

"Alms, alms," I cry, extending my hands like a helpless child. "Alms for the blind."

"Shame, shame," they whisper, their garments swishing by. "What shame hides in your family that God has cursed you so harshly?"

"Alms," I cry, my expression unchanging. Sometimes I think I would welcome deafness as well.

"No alms for you, uncle! I will not risk God's wrath."

The men often spit in the dust by my beggar's cup and try to fool me into reaching for a coin. When I was 13, a man tried that. I reached toward the spot where I'd heard the spittle land, only to discover a small warm glob of mud.

"Shame, shame!" I heard the man who'd spit at me laugh as he pulled his donkey forward. I longed to spit back at him but knew I'd probably hit a bystander instead. After that I reached forward only when I recognized the heavy soft *plunk* of a coin against the dust.

It came very rarely.

To pass the sweaty hours by this road, I live

through others' conversations. I hear patches of dialogue and invent bodies and hearts and lives for each voice.

"We must buy cheese today, Esther."

"Yes, Mama. Our goat has been so—"

"Isaac! Do not torture the donkey!"

"How far until the next village?"

"Oh, how I long for a drink!"

"Have you met this Jesus fellow?"

"No, but my aunt in Galilee has heard Him preach. Like a witch-man, they say. He holds you captive with His words of hope."

"Are they false?"

"I do not know, my friend. I do not know."

"They say He heals as well."

Like the leaves that often blow against my robes, the conversations approach, tug at my soul, and vanish forever. One topic, however, surfaces again and again. Jesus, this Man of Nazareth, who accuses the Pharisees and heals on the Sabbath.

I wonder about Him. I've long since refused to feel anything beyond hunger, thirst, and fatigue. But I wonder just the same. If He heals deaf-mutes and resurrects the dead, maybe this Man is genuine. At home I ask my coughing father what Jesus of Nazareth wants to do with us.

"Why, save us, of course!" he wheezes from his corner. "He claims a direct lineage back to David, and another honor as well."

"Yes?" I cease my rocking by the door and turn toward his voice.

"He says He is the Messiah."

I offer no comment, but my father's words sear like fire on softest skin.

Days pass, and I do not hear this Man pass with them. I push His existence to the back of my mind and concentrate on ignoring the taunts of the travelers.

One day, however, I sense a change. The people pay no mind to my wheedling. They rush instead toward some unspecified meeting place.

"He is coming!" they shout to one another in glee. "This Jesus is coming to our city!"

I pretend I haven't heard. I go on singsonging for alms as usual. But by midmorning my facade becomes impossible.

"He comes!" The cry arises from a press of people inching forward in the dust. I shut my mouth and strain to hear His voice. Just His voice would satisfy my curiosity.

"I have brought my Elijah. He shakes and slobbers like a madman. I know Jesus will heal him." The woman's voice rings through the noise.

Jesus does more than simply speak. He heals!

I slouch down into my folded arms. He will never see me—will He?

"Make way. Make way, people. Jesus must breathe too, you know. Make *way*, I say!" A rumbly voice rises above the crowd. His servant, perhaps?

"Peter, not so gruff. Look! There is a sad little girl. Bring her to me. Now, princess, what's the trouble? Shall I tell you a story?"

Jesus! This is the voice of Jesus! I know it instinctively, and I can't stop what happens if my life depended on it.

"Jeeeeeeesus! Jeeeeeesus! Jeeeeeesus, Son of David, have mercy on me!" A voice begins to wail, high and weak, and I faintly recognize it as my own. "Jeeeeeeesus, Jeeeeeeesus! Jeeeeeee—"

From the blackness a wide salty hand clamps over my mouth. "Quiet, you fool! He has no money for hungry blind men!" I recognize the voice of the one He calls Peter hissing down at me. He doesn't understand. It isn't alms I want.

"Bring him here," Jesus' voice calls, ahead of me and to the right.

I hear no other words. Before the fish-smelling Peter can lift me up, I thrust his meaty arm aside and stand to my feet. Hands outstretched, I walk toward the memory of His voice. Once again I feel like a helpless begging child.

"What is it you want?" His voice asks me softly.

I gulp. I, Bartimaeus, stand in the presence of Jesus! The Messiah! I give Him my faith with the joyful abandon that a child had once given his only coin to me. "Master, I wish to see!"

Even before the strange whiteness seeps into my head, I know He will heal me. I blink. In front of me words issue from a face I finally see.

"Your faith has healed you. Go in peace."

And then the crowd is upon Him again. "Master! Heal my blind boy!"

"I have an uncle sick these four years. Will You come?"

But I hear their pleas only dimly. As a crowd of burly men guide Him away, Jesus looks over His shoulder at me and shows me the first smile I have ever seen.

I can not resist. Stumbling, clawing, stepping over shadows and staring at the sky, I follow Him down the road.

I've heard His message this day. The men on the road were right. He holds me captive with His words. But I do not mind. There will be time later to explain to my father and mother. Now I want to learn all I can from this strange Galilean. By sunset—the first I have ever known and one that makes me cry—I have found a faith so fresh I want to burst with the joy of it. I walk home in the dark, following the familiar path by feel, even though my eyes are open.

"I can see," I whisper to myself and to the world. "I can see this God who heals both body and spirit. And I will follow Him."

Reference Points:

"Open my eyes that I may see wonderful things in your law" (Psalm 119:18).

"Then they came to Jericho. As Jesus and his disciples, together with a large crowd, were leaving the city, a blind man, Bartimaeus (that is, the Son of Timaeus), was sitting by the roadside begging. When he heard that it was Jesus of Nazareth, he began to shout, 'Jesus, Son of David, have mercy on me!' Many rebuked him and told him to be quiet, but he shouted all the more, 'Son of David, have mercy on me!' Jesus stopped and said, 'Call him.' So they called to the blind man, 'Cheer up! On your feet! He's calling you.' Throwing his cloak aside, he jumped to his feet and came to Jesus. 'What do you want me to do for you?' Jesus asked him. The blind man said, 'Rabbi, I want to see.' 'Go,' said Jesus, 'your faith has healed you.' Immediately he received his sight and followed Jesus along the road" (Mark 10:46-52).

"Jesus replied, 'Go back and report to John what you hear and see: The blind receive sight, the lame walk, those who have leprosy are

cured, the deaf hear, the dead are raised, and the good news is preached to the poor'" (Matthew 11:4, 5).

"He heals the brokenhearted and binds up their wounds" (Psalm 147:3).

"I am the Lord, who heals you" (Exodus 15:26).

Chapter Twenty-three

God *of Unity*

"Mark time, *march!*" Mr. Heagy's voice halts our straggling parade across the sand. I look over at Charley and roll my eyes. Nothing like drill team practice to get your adrenaline pumping.

"Halt!"

Just in time I cease my robotic movement and snap to attention.

"At ease."

An audible sigh of relief ascends from our five-person drill team. During ninth grade in a one-room school, Pathfinders seems surprisingly corny.

"Now, how can we improve our performance?" Mr. Heagy asks coolly, strutting around our raggedy ranks and appraising our form.

"Get a routine," Ryan quips dryly.

Carrie snickers.

"We will," Mr. Heagy promises. "But what can we work on right now? What do we need to practice?"

"Well," Jesse begins, smirking in my direction, "I think it would help if we *all* turn the right direction when you say 'right face.'"

"Hey, don't laugh! I was thinking about something else!" I punch him in the arm.

"Actually, Jesse's right," Mr. Heagy interrupts.

I slouch back into position.

"We could also improve our synchronization. Some people are shorter than others, you know."

Charley hangs his head. "Sorry. I'll slow down."

"Good. Now, let's march around the driveway again." Mr. Heagy claps his hands and assumes his military pose—hands behind his back, chin an extra two inches in the air. "Atten-*hut!* Forward *march!* Left . . . left . . . left, right, left . . ."

Amid good-natured groans, our drill team shuffles around that dusty driveway *again,* and I let my mind wander to the upcoming Pathfinder camporee. *Ryan was right. We haven't started working on our routine yet, and we're running out of time. I hope we're ready for the big day.*

We practice another hour, and by the drill session's conclusion, tempers flare as easily as the dust puffs beneath our hard-pounding feet.

"Hey, watch your step! That was my *heel*, you know!"

"Charley, pay attention! We stopped marching five minutes ago! Hel-*lo!*"

"Aw, do we have to practice that *again?* My feet are sore. Let's quit, OK?"

The next day, though, we're back at the school driveway, brainstorming for our routine.

"What should we do?" I wonder out loud. "I've never been on a drill team before."

"Yeah, and it shows," Jesse snickers beside me.

"Well, I have an idea." Mr. Heagy cuts in before I can deliver the usual punch in the arm. "Why not do the entire drill in silence? You can memorize the commands, so all I'll have to say is 'forward march.' What do you think?"

"Not bad," Charley offers. "But it will take a lot of work."

"And a lot of dedication, too. Are you prepared?"

We nod. "Just as long as we don't look stupid." Ryan speaks for all of us.

Yeah, right! I think as we scuffle into formation. *We're going to look stupid no matter what we do, wearing those dorky matching shirts and staring straight ahead like morons.*

I soon discover that the team shares my sentiments.

"I can't help it!" Carrie protests when Mr. Heagy asks her to pick up her feet. "That's the way I *walk!* Do you want me to look exactly like everyone else?"

"No," he says thoughtfully. "But I do want you to look synchronized."

"Why can't we all do our own thing?" Ryan demands. "I feel like a fool!"

"Because," Mr. Heagy explains for the fourth time that afternoon, "the object of a drill team is precision. You *would* look like a fool if you marched all by yourself."

"Maybe I just won't march at all," Ryan mutters darkly, scuffing a rock across the driveway.

But on the day of our presentation, the drill team remains intact.

"I'm nervous," I confess to Carrie, readjusting the sleeves on my field uniform. "What if I mess up?"

Carrie laughs. "Don't worry. That's why we perform as a group. It's not as obvious when you mess up in a crowd!"

"And now, from Tonasket, Washington, the Timber Wolves!" A man with a loudspeaker motions us onto the parade area. "Good luck, kids. You may begin."

"Pathfinders, atten-*hut!* Forward *march!"*

At Mr. Heagy's command our team snaps to life. *Left . . . left . . . left, right, left.* I hear Mr. Heagy counting out the cadence even though he stands silently at the end of the field. *Triple-to-the-right-flank, triple-to-the-left-flank, triple-to-the-rear march!* In near-perfect synchronization the Tonasket Timber Wolves execute their routine. Conversations quiet as people strain to see our performance.

"Halt."

Amid enthusiastic applause we walk, bashful and proud, from the field.

Needless to say, the drill team becomes suddenly uncorny. We review our routine for days after the performance.

"That wasn't so bad, was it?" Mr. Heagy asks Ryan the next week.

He shrugs and stares at the floor. "Nah. In fact, it was kinda fun."

I couldn't agree more fully.

Often I feel the same sentiments about the church. I'm tired of walking into a building, stuffed with the same people, and listening to the same philosophies rehashed each year. *Who says I have to believe that?* I ask myself again and again. *Who says that's the truth? In fact, who says I have to come to church at all?*

But I don't *have* to believe anything. Just as Mr. Heagy didn't make me march on the drill team, God doesn't force me to see things His way. However, I'm a part of this church because I chose it. I learned what I believed and found it to be in harmony with the church's beliefs—or at least I should have.

But I have to be honest. My individualistic spirit rebels against conforming to anyone else's beliefs.

Once again I'm drawn to the memory of that drill team. I didn't relish the thought of "copying" everyone else's actions any more than Ryan did. But when it came right down to it, we really weren't copying each other. We were acting out the marching orders Mr. Heagy gave us, doing everything we could to give them the beauty and precision that comes from working as a group. Performing the routine alone wouldn't have gained any recognition for either beauty or precision—in fact, it would have been almost pointless!

Still, it seems like so much more fun to blaze my own trail through life. Why must I belong to a group in order to act out my faith? I don't have to belong to any group. But as Carrie observed, it sure helps to have some support around when you make a mistake! I believe church exists for support as much as for action. When lovers of truth come together to worship and serve, they strengthen each other and offer a security that doesn't exist in solitude.

"May they be brought to complete unity," Jesus prayed before He left this earth (John 17:23). "That all of them may be one, Father, just as you are in me and I am in you. May they also be in us so that the world may believe" (verse 21). The kind of unity that God the Father and God the Son experience is whole unity—unity of purpose, spirit, and action. If I, as a member of the church, can intensify some of that purpose, spirit, and action here on earth, I will have experienced the power of the church.

When I think of the church in this light, I don't mind marching in cadence with a group of people. I realize now that I can still retain my individuality while upholding unity. God, who knows the true meaning of the word unity, wants me to experience the power and support it can provide.

Reference Points:

"My prayer is not for them alone. I pray also for those who will believe in me through their message, that all of them may be one, Father, just as you are in me and I am in you. May they also be in us so that the world may believe that you have sent me. I have given them the glory that you gave me, that they may be one as we are one: I in them and you in me. May they be brought to complete unity to let the world know that you sent me and have loved them even as you have loved me" (John 17:20-23).

"I will walk among you and be your God, and you will be my people" (Leviticus 26:12).

"Ruth replied, 'Don't urge me to leave you or to turn back from you. Where you go I will go, and where you stay I will stay. Your people will be my people and your God my God'" (Ruth 1:16).

"There are different kinds of gifts, but the same Spirit. There are different kinds of service, but the same Lord. There are different kinds of working, but the same God works all of them in all men. Now to each one the manifestation of the Spirit is given for the common good. To one there is given through the Spirit the message of wisdom, to another the message of knowledge by means of the same Spirit, to another faith by the same Spirit, to another gifts of healing by that one Spirit, to another miraculous powers, to another prophecy, to another distinguishing between spirits, to another speaking in different kinds of tongues, and to still another the interpretation of tongues. All these are the work of one and the same Spirit, and he gives them to each one, just as he determines. The body is a unit, though it is made up of many parts; and though all its parts are many, they form one body. So it is with Christ. For we were all baptized by one Spirit into one body—whether Jews or Greeks, slave or free—and we were all given the one Spirit to drink" (1 Corinthians 12:4-13).

Chapter Twenty-four

God *of the Committed*

Once upon a time two dusty travelers met in an old hotel.

"Gustav!" cried the first man, who had arrived just that day.

"Lars!" exclaimed the second fellow.

They slapped each other roughly on the back in the fashion of men who feel emotions too strong to express.

"I have not seen you for many years," Gustav said. "What brings you this way?" He motioned Lars toward a long bench by the fireplace.

Lars moved closer but hesitated to sit down, even when Gustav plopped down on the sturdy brown bench and propped his thick legs on an old log end. He studied his large roughened hands a moment before replying. "I cannot stay long, Gustav. I am on a journey, and my destination is far from here. I am going to the Great Hotel. Have you seen it?"

Gustav frowned, his bushy blond eyebrows coming together like two hurrying caterpillars. "No. I too search for that hotel. But I'll never find it. It lies so far away!"

"Surely you want to meet the Traveler who lodges there!" Lars asked quickly. "No matter how long the journey, I'm willing to make it for the honor of seeing this Man."

Gustav shook his head. "It's not that simple! Just because this Man has traveled the road before does not make the journey easy. I stopped here last year to repair a broken walking stick and haven't left since."

"But the Traveler—" interrupted Lars, a faraway shine tinging his gray-green eyes.

"Yes, yes," Gustav replied. "I too wish to know Him. But He is so very far away! What interest could this great Traveler possibly take in Gustav, a poor farmer?" He sighed and stared at the stones set around the fireplace. "I feel alone, my friend, and I do not know what to do. I'm tired of this hopelessness. I have no energy to travel. I wonder if I can ever be near enough to learn from Him."

"Of course you can!" Lars stomped a big boot emphatically, sending a small cloud of dust puffing to the ceiling. "I have told you the solution. Continue your journey toward the Traveler, and you *will* find Him!"

Gustav's expression didn't change. He stared into a discouragement Lars couldn't fathom. "He is far, so very far. I do not know what to do," he repeated softly, unheeding of Lars's advice. "What must I do?"

Lars looked down at the top of Gustav's head. Even his clumsily parted hair seemed discouraged. "I cannot help you any further," he finally decided. "I have told you all I know. If you wish to meet the Traveler, you must make the effort to reach Him. Sitting alone by this fire will never bring you closer. Use some effort, man!" Lars paused. No response from his friend. "Well, Gustav, I must continue this journey. Will you not come?" He waited, overcoat in hand, but Gustav didn't budge.

"Goodbye then," Lars sighed. "I pray you resume your journey soon."

Gustav made no reply. Beside the fireplace he stared at the flames and wished he could meet the Traveler without making the journey. *Is there no other way?* he wondered glumly, as the clock on the wall ticked off another hour of waiting solitude.

Meanwhile, Lars traveled directly toward the Man, the Traveler who knew the true meaning of the word commitment, with a dedication Gustav could not fathom.

Reference Points:

"Still another said, 'I will follow you, Lord; but first let me go back and say good-by to my family.' Jesus replied, 'No one who puts his hand to the plow and looks back is fit for service in the kingdom of God'" (Luke 9:61, 62).

"Those who suffer according to God's will should commit themselves to their faithful Creator and continue to do good" (1 Peter 4:19).

"In all my prayers for all of you, I always pray with joy because of your partnership in the gospel from the first day until now, being confident of this, that he who began a good work in you will carry it on to completion until the day of Christ Jesus" (Philippians 1:4-6).

"Jesus replied: '"Love the Lord your God with all your heart and with all your soul and with all your mind." This is the first and greatest commandment'" (Matthew 22:37, 38).

Chapter Twenty-five

God *Who Accepts*

"That should do it." I drop the last garbage bag into a rusty barrel and plod toward my cabin. After several weeks of counseling, I can hardly imagine another. But the kids will arrive at any minute, and I've already cleaned my cabin in preparation. There's nothing left to do but await their invasion.

I stand in my cabin's low doorway and survey the room with pride. *It won't stay clean for long,* I think as I flop down on my plastic-coated mattress. *And it won't stay quiet for long either.*

"Are you the Commanche counselor?" A small voice rouses me several minutes later.

I sit up quickly, already wearing a pasted-on smile. "I sure am! You must be one of my kids!"

The girl nods and steps inside. "Can I pick any bunk I want?"

"Excuse me, is this my daughter's cabin? Please find her a better mattress! This one is atrocious!" A red-haired mother stomps in and demands attention.

"Hey, over here! I need help with my sleeping bag!" Before long my cabin overflows with parents, campers, and a wide array of luggage. I rush from bunk to bunk, praying the week will speed by quickly. Only one bed left to fill. . . .

"This is it!" A gravely voice grinds through the chaos. I turn in time to see a woman with short-cropped hair lead both her husband and her daughter through the door. "Mandy, come here. Put your stuff right there. Be good while we're gone. We'll miss you. Goodbye."

In a series of staccato sentences she makes her departure. A quick hug seals the parting. Her husband reaches down as well, but Mandy stiffens and steps away. He holds up his hands in defeat and follows his wife from the cabin. "Be a good girl," he calls over a meaty shoulder.

I sigh. Merely watching the exchange makes me tired. Mandy, free from her parents, turns to me with a smirk. "You my counselor?"

I nod. We regard each other across the noisy cabin. Big for her age (which must be at least 13), Mandy is heavyset and pale. Her blond hair hangs in greasy clumps from beneath a tattered baseball cap. Her faded blue eyes flicker in and out of eye contact with me.

I finally break our silence. "My name is Sarah. I'm glad you're a Commanche this week."

Again she offers that formidable smirk. "Mandy," she says simply, extending a grubby hand. Her handshake tweaks a nerve in my arm and sends a painful tingle clear up to my neck. "Just call me Man."

I nearly choke. What 13-year-old would willingly call herself Man? For the next few hours I worry that she might have homosexual tendencies, but Man quickly proves her female identity. Before the night's conclusion she establishes herself as the oldest and most experienced girl in the cabin.

"Oh, I miss my boyfriend!" she whines after campfire. "He's so fine! Tommy and me, we're never apart!"

The girls rolls their eyes.

"We're going steady!" she continues, oblivious to their distaste. "Oh, I miss him so much!"

"And I miss my mommy," a pigtailed girl sighs from her bunk.

Man ignores her. "Last time I saw Tommy we sneaked into school after dark. It was so fun! He grabbed me and—"

"How long have you been going out?" I interrupt hastily. The girls' eyes tell me they wanted to hear the rest of Man's sentence, but I don't care.

"Two weeks." Man unzips her skintight jeans and glances around the room. "Turn around," she commands loudly. "I'm taking my clothes off for bed."

The dumbstruck girls obey, making faces at her behind their hands.

"Don't look!" Man shrieks at our backs. "I said don't look at me!"

I grin ruefully. It's going to be a tough week.

Several days later my prediction has already come true. Man has successfully turned every girl in the Commanche cabin into an enemy.

"She doesn't take showers," Missy complains one evening. "And she really stinks."

"Yeah, and she told us all about the gross things she does with Tommy," Jana adds. "I think she's yucky."

"Don't worry," I console. "I'll talk with Man as soon as I can."

But asking Man to shower is like begging a blue sky to rain. She smirks at me from beneath her baseball cap, her mousse-caked hair unmoving in the breeze. *Man obviously wants everyone to hate her,* I decide in frustration. *And she's succeeding with a flourish.*

"How can you stand her?" the other counselors ask me at staff worship. "She's a terror in every class, and a bully, too. I can't wait until she leaves!"

But Man stays. Apparently her parents have taken a monthlong vacation and left her at our mercy. Each week counselors pray that Man's name won't be on their new list of campers. She bounces from cabin to cabin like a one-person epidemic, leaving a wake of disillusioned counselors behind her.

By the fourth week I'm more than ready for Man's departure. Wherever she goes, cruelty follows like the flies that buzz around her head in morning worship.

"Girls, hurry up!" I call to my wandering charges.

They giggle and sidle closer to the line call area, pointing toward the boys' side of camp.

"Come on!" I brush a sweaty clump of hair from my eyes. "Hurry, or we'll be late again." As I turn around, I catch a glimpse of the Cherokee girls rushing toward line call. Man, holding her cap on with one hand, straggles far behind.

I cringe. Still an outcast. Yvonne, the Cherokee counselor, rolls her eyes as she hurries by. "It's almost over," she whispers gratefully. "No more Man!"

Just then Man spots me. The other girls have already rushed ahead and are greeting their friends at line call.

"Sarah!" she calls loudly, forgetting to hold her cap to her head. It nearly blows off as she runs toward me, and for the first time I see her whole head of hair. *Definitely. Keep the cap.*

I wave and step away. *Since when did you get so friendly?* I wonder. But before I can answer my own question, Man screeches to a stop and reaches out for a sweaty hug. "My friend Sarah," she whispers, wrapping her dusty arms around my neck and squeezing with all her might. Then, abruptly, she turns away.

As she shuffles toward her waiting cabin, I notice a shred of a smile slipping from her face. A smile! The first I've seen in a month! Dazed, I herd my own campers toward our spot in the line. What made Man develop a sudden liking for me? And why am I so hesitant to accept her friendship?

I have no answer. But on the last day of camp, when Man approaches me again, I'm ready. She rams into me like a football player and holds on until I think I'll suffocate under her smell. "You're my favorite counselor," she whispers, and disappears onto a crowded bus.

I stare. Man is finally gone. Man, who hides her used sanitary napkins under rocks outside our cabin. Man, whose laundry has been washed only once in four weeks. Man, who talks about Tommy even during worships. Man, whom nobody likes. I shudder, remembering my ill-concealed disgust at her personal-made-public habits. *Does she think I like her? It's nearly impossible!*

But later I realize that in Jesus' eyes I'm more like Man than I care to admit. "For all have sinned and fall short of the glory of God" (Romans 3:23). *I* have sinned. I, who ignore Him every day. I, who revel in doing exactly what He tells me not to. I, who ask forgiveness only to turn and sin again. I, who am unchangeably human.

How can He accept me into His arms? If I shudder at Man, who smells of sweat and dust, how much more must He shudder at me, who reeks of unforgiven sins? What hope is there for one so eternally flawed?

But wait! There's more to my guilty verdict. "For all have sinned . . . and are justified freely by His grace through the redemption that came by Christ Jesus" (verses 23, 24).

Freely? I am justified freely? What kind of love freely accepts a stinking mass of humanity into redemption? Certainly not the kind of love I extended to Man. Certainly not any kind of love I can fathom. But I am glad, so very glad, that this love exists in my God, the God who welcomes all kinds of sinners into His open arms, regardless of their past. The God who accepts.

Reference Points:

"Love must be sincere. Hate what is evil; cling to what is good. Be devoted to one another in brotherly love. Honor one another above yourselves. . . . Bless those who persecute you; bless and do not curse. Rejoice with those who rejoice; mourn with those who mourn. Live in harmony with one another. Do not be proud, but be willing to associate with people of low position. Do not be conceited. . . . If it is possible, as far as it depends on you, live at peace with everyone" (Romans 12:9-18).

"When a man's ways are pleasing to the Lord, he makes even his enemies live at peace with him" (Proverbs 16:7).

"Forgive my hidden faults. Keep your servant also from willful sins; may they not rule over me. Then will I be blameless, innocent of great transgression" (Psalm 19:12, 13).

"Let no debt remain outstanding, except the continuing debt to love one another, for he who loves his fellowman has fulfilled the law. . . . Love does no harm to its neighbor. Therefore love is the fulfillment of the law" (Romans 13:8-10).

Chapter Twenty-six

God *of the Sabbath*

"Adventists believe that Jesus wants us to worship on the seventh day," I explain to Chris over the phone. "We believe it's something we should be willing to die for if we have to."

"Die for?" Chris explodes. "You believe God expects you to *die* for something as small as a 24-hour day of worship? I think God is bigger than a few picky rules, don't you?"

I stare straight ahead, not knowing how to respond. Truthfully, I often wonder the same thing. If my religion stresses freedom in Christ so strongly, why do all my friends see only the rules?

"I don't understand," I complain to Renee later that week. "The conversation Chris and I had about the Sabbath made me wonder: How could God expect that kind of obedience? Shouldn't Christianity be fun instead of restricting?" I pace the room, feeling caged-up already. *"Principle* is more important than anything else, right? And the *principle* of the fourth commandment is the idea that everyone should take one day from their week to worship God!"

Renee scrunches up her eyebrows and waits patiently for me to continue.

"What if I work every day of the week but Tuesday?" I demand. "Would it be so wrong to make Tuesday my Sabbath? I'll be giving one day to God, won't I? I'll still uphold God's principle. Is it fair of Him to demand that our worship be on one particular day, and that day only?" My energy spent, I flop down on Renee's tan-carpeted floor.

She switches off her computer screen, realizing any attempt at homework is useless. "I've wondered that too," she sighs. "It seems like such an unreasonable commandment. But do you know what I finally decided?"

"What?"

"I decided that even though I may not understand why God asks for that kind of obedience, I'm willing to give it. Look at the other nine commandments. They're all 'commonsense' commandments, right? We would probably obey them anyway."

I nod. *Thou shalt not kill . . . Thou shalt not covet . . .* Several commandments flash through my mind.

"If God chooses to make one of the ten a little harder to understand, I'll accept the fact that He has a bigger reason for what He's doing. Does that make sense?" Renee looks at me intently.

"I guess so. I mean, yeah, I think. But it *still* bothers me. While I'm worshiping on Sabbath in America, our friends in Africa may be worshiping on Sunday."

Renee sighs. "I don't know, Sarah. I honestly don't know. All I know is that I keep Sabbath because God said so, even if I don't completely understand it. I want to do what He says. And besides"—she grins down at me—"I love the Sabbath. Don't you?"

I reflect for a minute. *My friends don't understand it. I miss a lot of activities.* But images of church campouts and Friday night vespers and noisy potlucks flood my mind. I remember waking up to special radio programs on Sabbath morning. I recall the feeling of dropping all my stress on Friday evening when the sun finally set. I remember learning the fourth commandment when in kindergarten and being filled with awe that God cared enough to give us an entire day to spend with Him.

"Yeah," I finally reply. "Yeah, I love Sabbath too."

This discussion didn't end my confusion. I still wonder what I should and shouldn't do on Sabbath. I still miss out on things I'd like to do. And I still explain my religion to people who don't understand. But it's getting a little easier. I realize that even though I don't understand God's exact motives, I can still enjoy the benefits of an entire day to spend with Him, my God, the God of the Sabbath.

Reference Points:

"'If you keep your feet from breaking the Sabbath and from doing as you please on my holy day, if you call the Sabbath a delight and the Lord's holy day honorable, and if you honor it by not going your own way and not doing as you please or speaking idle words, then you will find your joy in the Lord, and I will cause you to ride on the heights of the land and to feast on the inheritance of your father Jacob.' The mouth of the Lord has spoken" (Isaiah 58:13, 14).

"By the seventh day God had finished the work he had been doing; so on the seventh day he rested from all his work. And God blessed the seventh day and made it holy, because on it he rested from all the work of creating that he had done" (Genesis 2:2, 3).

"Remember the Sabbath day by keeping it holy. Six days you shall labor and do all your work, but the seventh day is a Sabbath to the Lord your God. On it you shall not do any work, neither you, nor your son or daughter, nor your manservant or maidservant, nor your animals, nor the alien within your gates. For in six days the Lord made the heavens and the earth, the sea, and all that is in them, but he rested on the seventh day. Therefore the Lord blessed the Sabbath day and made it holy" (Exodus 20:8-11).

"Then he said to them, 'The Sabbath was made for man, not man for the Sabbath. So the Son of Man is Lord even of the Sabbath'" (Mark 2:27, 28).

"Anyone who enters God's rest also rests from his own work, just as God did from his. Let us, therefore, make every effort to enter that rest, so that no one will fall by following their example of disobedience" (Hebrews 4:9-11).

Chapter Twenty-seven

God *Who Overcomes*

It all began with a strange squeaking noise in the corner of my room.

"What's that?" I look up from a box of college clothes I'm trying to unpack.

The squeaking continues, coming from a spot I can't identify. After several minutes of silence, I keep unpacking. *Red sweater goes here, jeans go here, shoes in the closet . . .*

The closet!

Suddenly I pinpoint the noise's location. I jerk open my closet door and face a wall of hanging clothes and storage shelves. As if on cue, the noise returns.

"Charley!" I shriek. "We've got mice!"

He ambles into my room. "Why are you standing on the bed?"

I shiver. "Look in the closet. Look for yourself. And listen."

He laughs up at me, his blue eyes daring me to move. "Boy, that's a problem. You'll have to get those out of there."

"Me?" I yelp, grabbing at his arm as he leaves. "No way! You have to help me!"

Ten minutes later Charley and our dog, Dappy, uncover a mouse nest made of the remains of my beach towel. I groan and peer up at my shelf. "Where are they?"

Charley lowers a gift bag, filled with old graduation cards, to the floor. "Look for yourself." He steps quickly from the room.

I peer into the bag. Two adolescent mice stare back at me, their bulging red eyes pleading for mercy. *"Aaaaaauuuugh!* Get them out of here! Help! Help!"

So began my Summer of the Mice. I thought I'd seen the last of the hairy rodents when I emptied the bag in front of Dappy's hungry jaws, but their fun had just begun.

Scrabble. Scrabble-scrabble. Thump!

My eyes fly open in the darkness.

Scrabble-scrabble. Thump! Scrabble.

I groan and roll over, hoping this is just a recurring nightmare. But as I lie on the bed in my little writer's cabin, the noises continue.

Thump! Scrabble-scrabble.

I finally sit up in bed. "It's 2:00 in the morning! I'm trying to sleep!"

Scrabble-scrabble.

The walls come alive with unwanted noises—my first mouse must have invited its extended family over. *And you'll take them with you when you leave!* I vow angrily, groping for the nearest hard object in reach. I fumble into my prayer journal.

Bang! It crashes into the wall with all the force of my fury. Grandpa once told me that mice fall dead from fear at sudden noises. I imagine tiny mouse explorers dropping through their own tunnels and hitting the ground far below. *Gotcha!*

"And don't come back," I grumble, flopping back into my flannel sleeping bag.

Scrabble. Thump! Scrabble-scrabble.

By morning I've thrown every available object at my walls and ceiling, and still the mice live on. *Maybe they sleep during the day,* I muse when I return to write the next morning. But by then the mice have built an amusement park on the peak of my roof. I can hear them climbing to the top and tumbling down again. *I hope you get motion sickness,* I fume angrily.

Scrabble, scrabble, scrabble, scrabble . . . Thump, thump, thump, thump, THUMP!

I glare at my computer screen. "What *else* can go wrong?"

Gnaw. Gnaw-gnaw. Gnaw. GNAW! GNAW! ***GNAW!***

My mental picture of those mice now includes a new variety—the Killer Termite Mice, who specialize in attacking small houses and chewing them to the ground.

"Well, I'm not leaving!" I snap. "At least you can't eat my computer!"

In the weeks that follow, I grow acquainted with those mice on a personal level. Delicate squeaks from near the floor signify a new batch of babies. Orderly scrabbling noises indicate their discovery of the roof ridge. And, when I'm lucky, they settle down for 10-minute naps during the day.

"I can't stand it!" I complain one evening. "I sit out there all day and try to write, but every few minutes some mouse has a traumatic experience, and I lose my train of thought! I'm going crazy!"

Mom grins. "I think you should turn this curse into a blessing," she suggests. "Why don't you write about your mice?"

"Huh," I sniff. "It's no blessing, but I've already thought of that." *I'll write their obituaries!* I think darkly.

The mice haven't left. Honestly, I'm trying to look on the bright side. But to me, they're just a bunch of yellow-toothed invaders. In fact, as I write this story, one enterprising fellow is investigating a new corner of the house. *Very loudly.*

It takes a greater person than I to see the blessing in an invasion of rodents.

You may laugh as you read this story, but it is traumatic for me to tell. I'm immortalizing these pests forever! And I know they'll never thank me.

Why am I doing it then? Why write about my worst enemies? Because I've made a decision, and I figure I have to start somewhere: "If it is possible, as far as it depends on you, live at peace with everyone. Do not take revenge, my friends, but leave room for God's wrath, for it is written: 'It is mine to avenge; I will repay,' says the Lord. On the contrary: 'If your enemy is hungry, feed him; if he is thirsty, give him something to drink. In doing this, you will heap burning coals on his head.' Do not be overcome by evil, but overcome evil with good" (Romans 12:18-21).

I know mice aren't quite the same as fellow human beings, but the principle still works. When someone wrongs me, I can turn that curse into a blessing by returning the favor—with something nice instead. And although these mice will never know what I've done for them, a reasoning human certainly would.

It's not going to be easy, this "living at peace" with everyone. If it cost me this much emotional trauma to "heap coals of fire" on unsuspecting mice, I can only imagine how hard it will be later.

Later, when a friend talks about me behind my back. Later, when a teammate is cruel. Later, when a family member makes me angry. I know it's possible, though. Why? Because I have the best example in the universe to follow: a God who overcomes. And I know that He will help me overcome too.

Reference Points:

"But I tell you who hear me: Love your enemies, do good to those who hate you, bless those who curse you, pray for those who mistreat you. If someone strikes you on one cheek, turn to him the other also. If someone takes your cloak, do not stop him from taking your tunic. Give to everyone who asks you, and if anyone takes what belongs to you, do not demand it back. Do to others as you would have them do to you" (Luke 6:27-31).

"I have told you these things, so that in me you may have peace. In this world you will have trouble. But take heart! I have overcome the world" (John 16:33).

"This is love for God: to obey his commands. And his commands are not burdensome, for everyone born of God overcomes the world. This is the victory that has overcome the world, even our faith. Who is it that overcomes the world? Only he who believes that Jesus is the Son of God" (1 John 5:3-5).

"He who has an ear, let him hear what the Spirit says to the churches. To him who overcomes, I will give the right to eat from the tree of life, which is in the paradise of God" (Revelation 2:7).

Chapter Twenty-eight

God *Who Is Stronger Than Satan*

"Let's run over to the church to practice our speeches," Lisa suggests on the Sunday before Student Week of Prayer. "I could use some help with mine; how about you?"

"Definitely," I agree.

Soon we walk through the dusk with Jen and Charity toward our tiny campus church.

"Someone must be inside," Jen observes. "The lights are already on."

The steeple glows an eerie gold in the fading sunlight. As we enter, Grant's familiar voice echoes in the foyer. "Stick around," he invites. "I was just finishing up."

In a few minutes Grant leaves, and we stand alone in our familiar orange-and-brown sanctuary. I shiver. Although churches are supposed to be safe, I always feel uneasy when I walk into an empty one.

"Jen, do you want to go first?" Lisa interrupts our silence, settling herself on a front-row pew.

"Sure!"

Several devotional talks later, Charity volunteers to go next. "Hold on a second," she calls, heading for the back of the church. "I need to find the sound track I'm going to play before my talk." She stops by the locked-up sound booth and scowls. "I think it's in here somewhere."

We follow her to the back of the church and poke around the cabinet. "We might be able to pick the lock," she mumbles, poking a finger through the slightly opened top. "Let's keep looking."

I stand a little behind the group and wait for them to open the sound booth. I'm not very mechanical. My help wouldn't be—

"Guys. *Guys!"* Suddenly, my own voice breaks into their conversation. "Let's get out of here!" I insist, tugging on Jen's coat sleeve. "I just saw a face through the window." I head toward the front of the church, away from that thing I've just seen.

"What was it?" Lisa asks as I sink onto the platform steps.

I shake my head. "I really don't know." The image flashes across my mind again and again. "But I know it was real. Either there's a person in the lobby of the church, or—" The fear on my three friends' faces assures me that they understand my meaning.

"It was probably just a person," Jen agrees shakily.

I swallow as the image returns again. "Uh, I don't think so. What I saw—the face—was a person I know. And there's no way he could be here right now." I am terrified they will reject my statement. "I promise I'm not making this up," I plead. "I have a great imagination, but never once have I imagined people or—or demons. This was real."

They nod. "We believe you."

I feel tears pushing against the back of my eyes. "I can't go out there. I can't walk through that lobby," I repeat over and over. "What if it's still there? What if it wants to hurt us? What if—"

"Are you sure it was a demon?" Charity asks softly.

"Yes!" My vehement reply echoes off the brick walls surrounding us. I cover my face and heave deep tearless sobs. "I can't go through that lobby."

Beside me, Jen's body stiffens in fear, but she reaches for my hand and pulls me to my knees. "We should pray."

We kneel there, a small knot of humanity in front of rows of empty pews, and plead for protection. The longer we pray, the closer together we move, until I feel as though nothing can penetrate our circle.

"God, if there's anything on our hearts that separates us from You, show us now."

"God, take away this fear—and take away that demon."

"God, please keep Satan far away."

As we pray, old rafters creak and heating vents groan. The wind whips bushes against the walls and whirls around the steeple. I feel as though Satan's evil angels are standing just behind us, laughing at our terror. Often, in the middle of someone's prayer, I open my eyes and jerk my head around to see if something has entered the church with us.

Finally, after several hours, we open our eyes.

"Do you think you can leave now?" Charity wonders, carefully searching my face.

I look away. No! No! screams my heart. But I don't want to keep them here any longer. "Yeah. Uh, yeah. I can go now," I manage, swallowing another sob.

As we walk, arm in arm, away from that church and toward the lighted porch of our dorm, it takes all my courage to keep from running. I shudder to think that the demon might return.

"What should I do?" I ask my dad over the phone. I'm afraid to sleep. Afraid to walk alone. Afraid to do anything that might invite that awful image back into my mind.

He sighs. "I wish I were there right now. I know what you're going through. I—"

"Why did the devil pick me to torment?" I interrupt. "What if he tries to hurt me?" I feel the tears push to the surface again and try to smooth my squeaky voice.

"I wondered the same thing when a similar situation happened to me," Dad admits.

So I'm not alone!

"I learned, after living in torment for several months, that I had nothing to be afraid of." Before I can protest, Dad continues. "I mean it. If I let the devil intimidate me, I admit that he may be stronger than God. And that's a lie. If God even snapped His fingers at the devil, he would tuck his tail and run."

I giggle at the mental picture Dad has created. "But Dad, it's not easy to be that brave."

"No. And it wasn't for me, either. But when you think about the fact that you're *already* on the winning side, it gets a whole lot easier." He pauses. "I believe everything you told me, Sarah. The devil often uses familiar people to get to our emotions. But you *can't* live in fear of losing a battle that God has already won. You can't!"

Dad's words give me hope and enough courage to fall asleep peacefully. Why? Because he reminds me that I serve a powerful God. A God who has never known defeat. A God who will not let me down when I claim His promises. A God stronger than Satan and every last one of his evil angels.

Reference Points:

"No temptation has seized you except what is common to man. And God is faithful; he will not let you be tempted beyond what you can bear. But when you are tempted, he will also provide a way out so that you can stand up under it" (1 Corinthians 10:13).

"Watch and pray so that you will not fall into temptation. The spirit is willing, but the body is weak" (Matthew 26:41).

"All your pomp has been brought down to the grave, along with the noise of your harps; maggots are spread out beneath you and worms cover you. How you have fallen from heaven, O morning star, son of the dawn! You have been cast down to the earth, you who once laid low the nations! You said in your heart, 'I will ascend to heaven; I will raise my throne above the stars of God; I will sit enthroned on the mount of assembly, on the utmost heights of the sacred mountain. I will ascend above the tops of the clouds; I will make myself like the Most High.' But you are brought down to the grave, to the depths of the pit. Those who see you stare at you, they ponder your fate: 'Is this the man who shook the earth and made kingdoms tremble, the man who made the world a desert, who overthrew its cities and would not let his captives go home?'" (Isaiah 14:11-17).

"The devil, who deceived them, was thrown into the lake of burning sulfur, where the beast and the false prophet had been thrown. They will be tormented day and night for ever and ever" (Revelation 20:10).

Chapter Twenty-nine

God I Choose: Three Temptations

Temptation I:

What do you need most?

No, seriously. I'd like to know. What, at this very moment, do you need more than anything else? Food? Shelter? Money? Love? Happiness? I'm sure you need something.

Aha! You're not happy, are you?

Oh. Well, that's strange. I thought you were a Christian. But of course if you're *not* a Christian, I can understand—

You *are* a Christian? Then why do you need anything? Correct me if I'm wrong, but Mama always told me that Christians never lack for their basic needs. Wouldn't you say happiness is a basic need? If you're a *real* Christian, you should never be sad. Right?

I'll tell you what. I'm a pretty fair guy. I'd like to believe that you're a Christian. I really would. But I need some concrete proof. So if (and remember I said *if*) you really are a follower of Christ, why don't you just ask Him for whatever you need, and then snap your fingers? If you're a Christian, God will give it to you. Food. Shelter. Money. Love. Happiness. After all, a just God would never want His children to suffer. Right?

What's this? You're not going to try it? Well, why

not? I thought it was a nice test! A witty test, in fact. A test that even a 5-year-old could understand. If you're a Christian, you get what you want—I mean, *need*—from God. Believe me, I study you Christians. And I should know.

Well, if you want to be that way, then suit yourself. I wasn't asking you to sell your soul. I just wanted a little proof. Of course, if you don't have enough faith to try a simple experiment . . .

All right, all right! I'm going!

Temptation II:

Oh, it's been a day, hasn't it? I can tell by the look on your dog-tired face. You've been struggling and struggling, trying to make ends meet, and your day still isn't finished.

Tell you what. Why don't you take a little break? It's a great evening, and I'm sure the stars are out. You can get a good view of the city from the top of that hill. Come on. Come on; I don't bite. Just a few minutes to rest your mind.

Ah, isn't it lovely?

No, no, I was speaking of the city below, not the— Oh, yes, the stars. They are lovely too. But I must confess I brought you up here, my friend, to show you the view of these lights. Simply spectacular, isn't it?

Where is your home? Can you show me from here?

Ah. I see.

It's rather far from the center of things, isn't it? Rather in a shabby section of town. Aren't the houses on that street a little old, a little leaky, and a little cheap?

No, no, I don't mean to insult you. Stay a little longer, please. It's only that, well, I'll be frank with you. I've seen a lot of this world. And I must say I prefer a privileged life to a penny-pinching existence.

You do too? I never dreamed we'd have so much in common! This is exciting! You see, I've been looking for someone to share my life with—I mean, *really* share. To set up in a nice house with a great view, and own a fast car. You know, that sort of sharing. Philanthropy, I guess you'd call it. But I haven't found anyone who'll accept my offer. It's really quite generous. You can have your own pool, you can get your college education for free, you can even buy your dad a sports car. Imagine the opportunities!

I know, I know. It's wonderful. And it could all be yours if—

No, I'm not a retired game show host. Allow me to finish.

It could all be yours if . . . you consent to do whatever I ask.

No, wait! I don't mean slavery! That went out of vogue years ago! I'm speaking of a business agreement. I'm the boss; you're not. Of course, I wouldn't ask you to do anything you didn't feel comfortable with. Strictly on your terms. In fact, the agreement is a mere formality—just a crutch to hang my generosity on. So people won't talk too much, you know. Just sign on the dotted line . . .

Come back! This is the chance of a lifetime! What? Christians don't obey anyone but God? Then why did you come up on this hill when I asked you to? I've got you there!

Come back, you little hypocrite! You're throwing away a bright future! Oh, believe me, you will live to regret this!

Temptation III:

Hey! Hey, you!

Yes, *you*. The good-looking, going-somewhere one. Come here for a second. I—I saw you in church the other day. You must be a Christian.

Good. I've been looking for someone like you.

You see, I've struggled with this for a long time. If you Christians are so sure that God exists, and if you really want others to follow Him too, it seems like you're missing something.

You're missing sensation.

No, not the chorus-girl, horror-story, dinosaur-movie kind of sensation. More of a, well, a conviction kind of sensation. You know, a boy-I'm-glad-I-follow-such-a-great-God kind of sensation.

What? Your God *is* great? Yes, well, how do *I* know that?

No, no, personal stories don't work anymore. Today's public needs concrete evidence. They need examples that happen right before their eyes, not conversion stories from five years ago. Let's face it. People today aren't as trusting as they used to be.

That's why I was thinking . . . Well, I have this idea that might help you win some souls . . .

What? Why do I want to help you? Oh, I don't know. I'm just a do-gooder, I guess. Anyway, here's the idea. If you, the never-takes-risks person that you are, really wanted to shine for Jesus, you could do something that would prove how much you trusted Him. Something really sensational. And then when He saved you, you'd be surrounded by crowds of weeping people, all begging for baptismal classes, thanks to you.

What should you do? Well, I was thinking of something rather tame for a start. Perhaps if you, say, yelled, "I trust my Jesus!" and ran across a rush-hour freeway you would attract a little attention.

No, no, you *wouldn't* need to be peeled off 17 cars and sewn back together. Don't you see? You'd emerge unscathed, and the masses would flock to your door, raising their hands in praise to God. Isn't it glorious? And then, after that, you could try camping in a military training zone. Or the Empire State Building.

Hey! I was just getting warmed up! What's wrong? Are you scared? Scared to take a chance for this God you talk so highly of? That's it, isn't it? You're just afraid! You don't believe He could protect you! Well, I know your kind. And I pity you. You'll never convince anyone that you're a true Christian.

What? Don't test the Lord your God? You choose *Him* over me? Well, what's that supposed to mean? I wasn't asking to *own* you or anything—not *exactly,* anyway.

OK, fine. Send me away. But I'm warning you, you'll see me again soon. I can't believe you call yourself a Christian. Watch out for me, "Christian." Because I'll be back before you know it.

Reference Points:

"Then Jesus was led by the Spirit into the desert to be tempted by the devil. After fasting forty days and forty nights, he was hungry. The tempter came to him and said, 'If you are the Son of God, tell these stones to become bread.' Jesus answered, 'It is written: "Man does not live on bread alone, but on every word that comes from the mouth of God."' Then the devil took him to the holy city and had him stand on the highest point of the temple. 'If you are the Son of God,' he said, 'throw yourself down. For it is written: "He will command his angels concerning you, and they will lift you up in their hands, so that you will not strike your foot against a stone."' Jesus answered him, 'It is

also written: "Do not put the Lord your God to the test."' Again, the devil took him to a very high mountain and showed him all the kingdoms of the world and their splendor. 'All this I will give you,' he said, 'if you will bow down and worship me.' Jesus said to him, 'Away from me, Satan! For it is written: "Worship the Lord your God, and serve him only."' Then the devil left him, and angels came and attended him" (Matthew 4:1-11).

"Have I not commanded you? Be strong and courageous. Do not be terrified; do not be discouraged, for the Lord your God will be with you wherever you go" (Joshua 1:9).

"Who is this King of glory? The Lord strong and mighty, the Lord mighty in battle. Lift up your heads, O you gates; lift them up, you ancient doors, that the King of glory may come in. Who is he, this King of glory? The Lord Almighty—he is the King of glory" (Psalm 24:8-10).

"Be strong and take heart, all you who hope in the Lord" (Psalm 31:24).

"Strengthen the feeble hands, steady the knees that give way; say to those with fearful hearts, 'Be strong, do not fear; your God will come, he will come with vengeance; with divine retribution he will come to save you'" (Isaiah 35:3, 4).

Chapter Thirty

God *Who Gives*

We wander around the used CD shop, lost in colorful aisles of music. I open a Newsboys CD cover. "Five ninety-nine!" I gasp. "That's nothing!"

Jon laughs. "They're all that cheap."

I grin and start down the aisle with a new resolve. *Time to boost my CD collection!*

"What about these?" I hold out the three CDs I've painfully chosen from at least 20 I want to purchase.

"Looks good," Jon replies. "I got three too." He shows me the alternative albums he's selected. "That is, if . . ." His voice trails off.

"Sure, I'll pay for them. Just don't forget to pay me back," I warn, opening my checkbook. "I'm in college too, you know."

"No problem."

Several weeks later, however, Jon still hasn't repaid his debt. "Where is it?" I fume, glancing at the balance on my newest bank statement. "I'm running out of money!"

"Why don't you just ask Jon about it?" Angie, who has patiently listened to my tirade, finally speaks.

"No, I don't want to make a big deal. Besides, Jon should remember by himself. That's what good friends do, right?"

She nods. "I thought so."

Good friends lend money. Good friends share their old clothes with you. Good friends help out with gas on a long trip. And good friends always pay back what they borrow.

Always? How does this philosophy work with Jesus? When He gives me peace, I can't return it to Him. When I ask for a favor and He does it, how can I repay Him? When He provides me with extra money, extra time, or extra happiness, how can I show my gratitude? Since I can't measure out what He's given me and send the same quantity back to Him, there must be something else I can do. I want to be a good friend.

I believe we can repay God by using our blessings to make other people happy. If, for instance, He blesses me with peace, I can spread that peace among my friends, helping them find the same rest in God that I've found. If He blesses me with money or time, I can show my gratitude by donating some of that money or time to help others. And if He blesses me with a particular talent, it's my responsibility to use that talent to honor Him. Malachi sends a direct warning from God:

"'If you do not listen, and if you do not set your heart to honor my name,' says the Lord Almighty, 'I will send a curse upon you, and I will curse your blessings. Yes, I have already cursed them, because you have not set your heart to honor me'" (Malachi 2:2).

In other words, it's my duty to honor God with my blessings. It's not enough to accept a favor without saying thank you. God expects more.

God who? God the Giver; the one who supplies me with all sorts of incredible gifts—and then waits to see exactly how I'll disperse them again to show my gratitude.

Reference Points:

"Give, and it will be given to you. A good measure, pressed down, shaken together and running over, will be poured into your lap. For with the measure you use, it will be measured to you" (Luke 6:38).

"The God who made the world and everything in it is the Lord of heaven and earth and does not live in temples built by hands. And he is not served by human hands, as if he needed anything, because

he himself gives all men life and breath and everything else. From one man he made every nation of men, that they should inhabit the whole earth; and he determined the times set for them and the exact places where they should live. God did this so that men would seek him and perhaps reach out for him and find him, though he is not far from each one of us. 'For in him we live and move and have our being.' As some of your own poets have said, 'We are his offspring'" (Acts 17:24-28).

"I will bless them and the places surrounding my hill. I will send down showers in season; there will be showers of blessing" (Ezekiel 34:26).

"Therefore, since we are receiving a kingdom that cannot be shaken, let us be thankful, and so worship God acceptably with reverence and awe" (Hebrews 12:28).

Chapter Thirty-one

God *Who Forgives*

(Based on Luke 22:54-62; John 21:15-19)

"I'm sorry" wouldn't cut it. In fact, a million "I'm sorrys" wouldn't even come close. What I did was so bad that words could never apologize it away. That's why, when I saw Him again, I didn't know what to do. It was on the beach, where we mostly hung out. Me and the boys were fishin', like usual. Only this time, we weren't catchin' a thing. We'd been out there all night, and I was so tired I kept seein' birds where there weren't no birds, and waves where there weren't no waves. I don't think any of us had slept too good since the day He died.

You gotta know I'm talkin' about Jesus, that long-haired Man from Galilee. You know, everybody's been in an uproar about His death. I know it wasn't fair. It made me madder than a donkey in a dust storm. But there was absolutely nothing anybody could do. He warned us He was gonna die, but none of us wanted to believe Him. Guess we just had it figured He would lead us right into victory against those no-good Romans.

Course we had Him figured all wrong. Jesus—He's better than a lot of political meddlin' and pokin' around. He wanted to do more than just save us Jews; He wanted to save the world. And you know what?

That's exactly what He did, the day He died.

I barely remember that day, 'cause from about dawn onward I was a complete mess. I'd just got through tellin' this guy I didn't give a fig who Jesus was when this big ol' rooster crowed right behind me.

And then I remembered what He'd said about me denyin' Him and about the old cock crowin' at dawn, and I near passed out on the spot.

Jesus—He's never wrong.

I did the thing that came most natural. I ran away. Far away as I could get from the fact that I'd just betrayed the greatest Man I knew. But every time I heard a rooster proclaim the mornin', I wanted to go out and drown myself. I was so miserable and so discouraged that I couldn't think of nothin' to do but fish.

Well, that's right where I found the rest of the boys. Guess those ol' boats were our unofficial meetin' spot. Nobody said much—just sorta picked up those nets and set in where we'd left off three years ago.

Anyway, along about mornin' we're workin' away quiet as a graveyard, haulin' in nothin' but an occasional weed of the sea, when this stranger happened by and, for the fun of it, asked us to fish on the wrong side of the boat. We was all in the mood for a laugh, so we tried it. And what do you know! The nets filled so full we could barely heave 'em into the boat!

And then I got this funny prickly feelin' on the back of my neck. I looked up at this laughin' stranger on the shore. My decision didn't take more 'n two seconds. I just hiked up my robe and ran through that shiver-cold water straight toward my Master. For a minute I forgot all about the fact that He should want to kill me for what I'd done. But later, when He asked me to go for a walk with Him, I knew I didn't even belong here. Didn't belong on this beach in the dawn, havin' a reunion with the Man I'd just betrayed. But I'd been runnin' for several days, and I was mighty tired of it. So I set off with Him down the shore.

"Peter," He finally said, starin' out to sea where the sun kinda made a million reflections on the waves.

I was too scared to do much more than squeak, but I managed to answer. "Yeah?"

"Peter, do you love Me?"

Now, I woulda washed His feet every day for the rest of my life. I woulda cleaned the dung from the streets of Jerusalem. I woulda gone singing to the dungeon if He asked me to. But no, He just asked me if I *loved* Him. That stung like a sea-swim on a sunburn, but I had to answer.

"I—I do, Lord." I couldn't apologize, or I woulda become a sobbin', quiverin' mess at His feet. Not a pretty sight.

Jesus considered the sunrise some more and I held my breath longer than a dead fish ever has. Finally He spoke. "Feed My lambs."

I just couldn't believe my ears. Jesus wanted me to work for Him again. I was still His disciple! I don't think He could believe His ears either, 'cause He asked me three times if I really loved Him. And each time hurt a little worse than the time before. Finally He looked away from that gray-gold sunrise on the water and stared at me instead. "Follow Me."

I poked my left leg with my right big toe to make sure I wasn't dreamin'. You see, that's exactly what Jesus told me the day we met. "Follow Me," He had said, and I did. And here He was, standin' with His nail scars on a soggy beach in front of the man who denied Him, askin' me to start over again!

Well, that did it. I forgot about the boys watchin' from the grill, and I dropped to my knees and became the tremblin', sobbin' mess I'd been scared to become.

You know, as I crouched there on that beach, I realized somethin' amazin'. I'd *always* been a tremblin', sobbin' mess inside. But you know what? He still wanted me!

See, I don't know how He done it, but Jesus musta seen right through my curses and jokes and mistakes to the fact that I really did care. And He forgave me for all my mess-ups and let me work for Him again.

I didn't deserve it. I even tried to tell Him that a few times. But He just looked at me; looked at me so hard I knew He could see how sorry I was; and I couldn't argue any more. 'Cause when He looks like that, I can see into Him too. And do you know what I saw that day? I saw the most amazin' and true kind of love I've ever known.

Yeah, Jesus forgave me completely. And here's why I'm tellin' you all about it.

I know. I know what it's like to feel that He could never want you back. And I know too that if Jesus my Master could want *me* back, then He could want *anyone* back. That's just the kind of guy He is. A God who loves to forgive.

Reference Points:

"Blessed is he whose transgressions are forgiven, whose sins are covered. Blessed is the man whose sin the Lord does not count against him and in whose spirit is no deceit" (Psalm 32:1, 2).

"When they had finished eating, Jesus said to Simon Peter, 'Simon son of John, do you truly love me more than these?' 'Yes, Lord,' he said, 'you know that I love you.' Jesus said, 'Feed my lambs.' Again Jesus said, 'Simon son of John, do you truly love me?' He answered, 'Yes, Lord, you know that I love you.' Jesus said, 'Take care of my sheep.' The third time he said to him, 'Simon son of John, do you love me?' Peter was hurt because Jesus asked him the third time, 'Do you love me?' He said, 'Lord, you know all things; you know that I love you.' Jesus said, 'Feed my sheep. I tell you the truth, when you were younger you dressed yourself and went where you wanted; but when you are old you will stretch out your hands, and someone else will dress you and lead you where you do not want to go.' Jesus said this to indicate the kind of death by which Peter would glorify God. Then he said to him, 'Follow me!'" (John 21:15-19).

"If we confess our sins, he is faithful and just and will forgive us our sins and purify us from all unrighteousness" (1 John 1:9).

"Jesus said, 'Father, forgive them, for they do not know what they are doing'" (Luke 23:34).

Chapter Thirty-two

God *Who Welcomes Me Home*

"I hate it here!" 7-year-old Carrie screamed at our class. "I'm going back to Colorado!" Flipping her long brown hair behind her, she marched to her desk and unloaded its contents onto the floor.

We watched in silence. This scene was a common occurrence. Carrie, recently arrived in Washington, spent most of her time reminding us that Colorado was a much better state. That she didn't like Washington weather. And that as soon as possible she would return "home."

We let her rave. As Carrie's pile of papers, markers, and textbooks grew, I realized that I didn't understand her unhappiness. I felt perfectly content right where I was.

"I'm making my parents take me home!" Carrie reminded us as she threw a ruler onto her going-to-Colorado pile.

But Carrie never moved back to Colorado. In fact, she and her family still live in Washington, and I'd venture to say she likes it better here than she did so many years ago. Now, 13 years later, I can finally identify with her frustration.

"I want to go home!" I complained to Lisa as we stumbled around our tiny lakefront room. "I like camp, but I hate my job!"

She rummaged through a drawer in search of her

staff T-shirt. "I know what you mean. I'm tired of cooking for picky kids."

"I wonder if we'll fix potato casserole again this week."

"Probably." Lisa wrinkled her nose. "I have the entire menu memorized!"

"I want to go home," I repeated softly, pulling on my right tennis shoe. "I can handle the work. But no matter what I do, I can't seem to get in touch with God while I'm here! I feel as though my environment is ruining my spirituality."

Lisa nodded. "Exactly. Do you feel like it's not your fault that you're so far away from God?"

"Uh-huh. I think a change of scenery would make all the difference in the world."

We pondered this dilemma in silence as we prepared for another day in the hot summer camp kitchen. Unfortunately, neither Lisa nor I found the solution that summer. We mixed and measured, sautéed and sliced, but never once stumbled on a good recipe to reduce our distance from God. Now, two summers later, we still describe that experience as one of the worst in our lives: the time when our environment dictated our spirituality.

It still bothers me. How could something as trivial as a bad job and no support group weaken my relationship with God? Could I have counteracted the negative environment I lived in? Shouldn't my faith be strong enough to survive, in spite of adverse circumstances?

Several weeks ago these questions surfaced again.

"I feel so far away from God," Chris admitted as we sat on a rock overlooking our hometown valley. "I think it's because of the time I spent at field training for ROTC. I just— I don't know. I didn't have a spare moment to spend with Him. And now that I have more time, I don't know what to do. I feel as though the situation really messed me up." He sighed and picked at the moss-covered rock we sat on. "Do you know what I mean?"

I nodded. *Did I know?* "Yeah, I understand." Suddenly curiosity overtook me. Maybe Chris could shed some light on my questions.

"But you can't change your environment, so it's not your fault. Right?" I threw the question out and waited for his response.

"I can't change my environment," he agreed, "but I think it was my fault too. If I want a good relationship with God, I should stand up to tough times instead of wimping out when the going gets tough."

I kicked at a shrub next to my legs. "But it's so frustrating! It seems that no matter what happens, I constantly fluctuate between a close friendship and a bad one with Him. Why can't I just stay stable?"

"I don't know, Sarah. I wish I could tell you."

I barely heard him. "It must have something to do with human nature. It's like we're attached to rubber bands whose other end hooks to God. When times are good and we're doing fine, we stretch the rubber band to its limit. We leave God completely alone."

"But when we're stressed out or lonely, we suddenly pull in closer to Him to give us support and strength," Chris interrupted. "I know, I know. It's like a cycle. And I *hate* it! Why can't I stay close to Him all the time?"

I thought for a minute, staring out at the darkening sky and the birds cartwheeling across it. "I think we already answered that, Chris. Because we're human, right?"

He sighed. "Yeah, I guess so."

"But," I began cheerfully, "God understands us! No matter how many times we let situations pull us away, He'll still accept us back again!"

Chris smiled, and I relaxed. There was hope after all. Hope that, even though I couldn't understand why I let my environment drag me down, God knew I was human. Hope that even though I made the same "rubber band" mistake again and again, He never tired of welcoming me home. Despite my inescapable human nature, I serve a God who forgives and understands. A God who, no matter how often I stray away, still welcomes me home.

Reference Points:

"The Lord appeared to us in the past, saying: 'I have loved you with an everlasting love; I have drawn you with loving-kindness'" (Jeremiah 31:3).

"In keeping with his promise we are looking forward to a new heaven and a new earth, the home of righteousness. So then, dear friends, since you are looking forward to this, make every effort to be found spotless, blameless and at peace with him" (2 Peter 3:13, 14).

"The eyes of the Lord are everywhere, keeping watch on the wicked and the good" (Proverbs 15:3).

"The heavens declare the glory of God; the skies proclaim the work of his hands. Day after day they pour forth speech; night after night they display knowledge. There is no speech or language where their voice is not heard" (Psalm 19:1-3).

"Submit yourselves, then, to God. Resist the devil, and he will flee from you. Come near to God and he will come near to you" (James 4:7, 8).

"Jesus continued: 'There was a man who had two sons. The younger one said to his father, "Father, give me my share of the estate." So he divided his property between them. Not long after that, the younger son got together all he had, set off for a distant country and there squandered his wealth in wild living. After he had spent everything, there was a severe famine in that whole country, and he began to be in need. So he went and hired himself out to a citizen of that country, who sent him to his fields to feed pigs. He longed to fill his stomach with the pods that the pigs were eating, but no one gave him anything. When he came to his senses, he said, "How many of my father's hired men have food to spare, and here I am starving to death! I will set out and go back to my father and say to him: Father, I have sinned against heaven and against you. I am no longer worthy to be called your son; make me like one of your hired men." So he got up and went to his father. But while he was still a long way off, his father saw him and was filled with compassion for him; he ran to his son, threw his arms around him and kissed him. The son said to him, "Father, I have sinned against heaven and against you. I am no longer worthy to be called your son." But the father said to his servants, "Quick! Bring the best robe and put it on him. Put a ring on his finger and sandals on his feet. Bring the fattened calf and kill it. Let's have a feast and celebrate. For this son of mine was dead and is alive again; he was lost and is found." So they began to celebrate'" (Luke 15:11-24).

Chapter Thirty-three

God *of Mercy*

(Based on Jonah 4)

"God, I wish I had some water. Just a mouthful. Just enough to get that awful dusty taste out of my mouth. I don't ask for much these days. Oh, God, wish I had some water."

You had enough water not long ago, Jonah.

"You always do that! You bring things up just to embarrass me! I *know* I had plenty of water several months ago. How could I forget?"

I was hoping you hadn't.

"You think I've forgotten my lesson? I remember, good and well. I remember the storm that sent those sailors into a panic. I remember the desperation on their faces as they hoisted me over the rail and dropped me into the sea. Did You think I was so callous?"

I was hoping you weren't.

"What is *that* supposed to mean? I'm not an unfeeling man. I'm really not. I *wept* for those people in Nineveh the first day I saw them."

Did you?

"Yes, as a matter of fact I did. I wept. And then I descended on the city like the cloud of judgment You asked me to be! I threatened them. I accused them. I uncovered their sinful ways. It was wonderful. I could feel Your righteous indignation as they groveled in ashes and begged for mercy."

Or was it your *righteous indignation?*

"Come on; You were angry too. You said You'd level the city."

Yes. But—

"But when the time actually came and I fled in terror, nothing happened."

Nothing, Jonah? You call the repentance of so many sinners nothing?

"You know what I mean. The city, God! The city stayed intact. I could hear the sound of their laughter clear out here in the desert. Laughter at Jonah and his message of folly."

What makes you so sure they weren't cheering with joy at being forgiven?

"God, I wish I had some water. This cursed heat—"

Jonah.

"Even the sun seeks to brighten my skin with a blush. I hate this spot. I am so angry I could die. I could just curl up right here and—"

Jonah.

"Yes, Lord?"

Look at the ground.

"What's this? You want me to notice a weed in the desert? Great. It's lovely. Now, as I was saying—"

Look again, Jonah.

"Well! It's grown past my knees already! It's up to my waist! It's—it's shoulder-high— No, wait! It's over my head! What kind of camel fertilized this soil?"

Recognize a miracle when you see one, Jonah?

"Well, it *is* kind of shady under this vine. I suppose I should say thank You. Yes, a vine is a wonderful trade for a lifetime of shame, isn't it? I do appreciate Your consideration. . . . God? God? God, can You hear me? I'm talking to You, God!

"Lost Him again. Well, this vine is nice, but I asked for water. Can't He get it straight? Water, vine—they don't even sound alike. God? God? . . . Fine. I'm going to sleep."

"Oh. Oh. This is just too much. I can't believe this. How long have I lain here, sweating in the sand, with no shade to protect me? How long?"

Not long enough to die, Jonah.

"You're back, are You? Well, I wish I had lain here longer, then. I'm ready to die."

Jonah—

"First You point me to Nineveh. Then You stuff me in a big fish. Then You point me to Nineveh again. Then You don't fulfill Your promise, and I look like a fool. Again. And *now* You can't even keep my vine alive! What kind of God would—"

I warn you. Be silent!

"___"

Very good. Now. Look at that vine.

"What's left of it, You mean."

You cared for it, did you not?

"Yes, I did."

You cared for it, Jonah. Yet you did not plant it. You did not water it. You did not stretch its roots downward nor pull its stem toward the sky.

"So?"

Jonah, Jonah! If you care so much for one vine, imagine how much more I care for each person in Nineveh. I love them, Jonah! Can't you see? I love them in a way you never can. I created them and nourished them more lovingly than a man nourishes his best-producing vine. Is there any reason I should not love these people enough to accept their repentance? Is there any reason to blot out an entire group of people, even though they are cleansed and repentant?

"___"

You cannot see, can you? You cannot see the love I hold for them and for you. I am your God, Jonah, though you are loath to admit it. I am your God, the God who formed you from birth and forgave your uncountable sins. I am your God, a God of eternal mercy.

Reference Points:

"For I will take you out of the nations; I will gather you from all the countries and bring you back into your own land. I will sprinkle clean water on you, and you will be clean; I will cleanse you from

all your impurities and from all your idols. I will give you a new heart and put a new spirit in you; I will remove from you your heart of stone and give you a heart of flesh. And I will put my Spirit in you and move you to follow my decrees and be careful to keep my laws" (Ezekiel 36:24-27).

"But Jonah was greatly displeased and became angry. He prayed to the Lord, 'O Lord, is this not what I said when I was still at home? That is why I was so quick to flee to Tarshish. I knew that you are a gracious and compassionate God, slow to anger and abounding in love, a God who relents from sending calamity. Now, O Lord, take away my life, for it is better for me to die than to live.' But the Lord replied, 'Have you any right to be angry?' Jonah went out and sat down at a place east of the city. There he made himself a shelter, sat in its shade and waited to see what would happen to the city. Then the Lord God provided a vine and made it grow up over Jonah to give shade for his head to ease his discomfort, and Jonah was very happy about the vine. But at dawn the next day God provided a worm, which chewed the vine so that it withered. When the sun rose, God provided a scorching east wind, and the sun blazed on Jonah's head so that he grew faint. He wanted to die, and said, 'It would be better for me to die than to live.' But God said to Jonah, 'Do you have a right to be angry about the vine?' 'I do,' he said. 'I am angry enough to die.' But the Lord said, 'You have been concerned about this vine, though you did not tend it or make it grow. It sprang up overnight and died overnight. But Nineveh has more than a hundred and twenty thousand people who cannot tell their right hand from their left, and many cattle as well. Should I not be concerned about that great city?'" (Jonah 4).

"Remember, O Lord, your great mercy and love, for they are from of old. Remember not the sins of my youth and my rebellious ways; according to your love remember me, for you are good, O Lord" (Psalm 25:6, 7).

"Let us then approach the throne of grace with confidence, so that we may receive mercy and find grace to help us in our time of need" (Hebrews 4:16).

"As for you, you were dead in your transgressions and sins, in which you used to live when you followed the ways of this world and of the ruler of the kingdom of the air, the spirit who is now at work in those who are disobedient. All of us also lived among them at one time, gratifying the cravings of our sinful nature and following its desires and thoughts. Like the rest, we were by nature objects of wrath. But because of his great love for us, God, who is rich in mercy, made us alive with Christ even when we were dead in transgressions—it is by grace you have been saved. And God raised us up with Christ and seated us with him in the heavenly realms in Christ Jesus, in order that in the coming ages he might show the incomparable riches of his grace, expressed in his kindness to us in Christ Jesus" (Ephesians 2:1-7).

Chapter Thirty-four

God I Praise

"This is great!" 18-year-old Jessica shouts to her friend Rick. "I've never been to a concert like this before!"

Dancing beside her, Rick grins broadly. Neither of them have experienced a mash pit at a Christian concert, but they're both thoroughly enjoying the experience. As they raise their arms in praise to God, Jessica can't help wondering what her church family would think of her behavior.

"I don't care," she decides. "This is the most heartfelt praise I've ever known. And nobody can take that away from me."

"I know it's not wrong," Mr. Thornton admits to his gray-haired wife. "But every time I see people clapping to religious music, it almost drives me crazy."

"Why?" she wonders, drying another dish and placing it in the cupboard.

"When I was in academy," Mr. Thornton explains, "some of the students got a little rowdy during assembly—clapping, stomping, that sort of thing. We didn't think it was wrong. But our principal stopped the entire meeting to warn us that the devil was in that place and that we were defying God Himself."

Mrs. Thornton looks up at him. "So now, even though it's accepted, clapping in worship seems like blasphemy?"

"Yes."

Fourteen-year-old Joel turns up the volume on his tinny car stereo. "Like my music?" he asks his backseat passengers.

They mouth something unintelligible and nod their heads.

"It's Christian, you know," Joel offers proudly. "I've changed my tastes."

Beside him, Lisa laughs. *Christian? This music is Christian?* She can hardly distinguish the words, let alone find any shred of praise in this ear-pounding music. In between songs she wonders if unrecognizable words qualify as music to God. She certainly doesn't think so.

Drums. Electric guitars. Noise. Raised hands. Body movement. Screaming. How many forms of music can be considered spiritually uplifting?

"Well, I certainly don't think anyone could praise God and listen to that music at the same time," asserts a matronly housewife. "I make my kids throw those tapes away if I find them."

"How could *anyone* get excited about that boring gospel stuff?" wonders an eighth-grade student after church service. "The words are *so* predictable, and there's no value in the same three chords repeated over and over. I hate it!"

"I'm tired of the same music," a young father complains to his wife. "I want a change, but I don't know what. And I don't know what's acceptable in our church either. I feel so stifled!"

From the wide spectrum of opinions represented in the church, a news reporter would think they were interviewing at least eight denominations instead of one! Is there a way to harmonize so many concepts of "praise"?

At a potluck service last spring, I think I found a beginning.

"Hey, let's go make some music!" Richard called to me from the emptying sanctuary.

I followed him inside. But instead of the usual small group of guitarists, a wide array of styles bombarded my ears. Brian, our pastor's son, sat hunched around an old acoustic guitar, crooning the words to an alternative Christian song. Bruce, our resident cowboy, fumbled with his mandolin and waited for someone to suggest a country tune. Richard, a seventies rock addict, thumped on his bass, tapped his feet, and tried to find the melody in Brian's music. And Grandma? Well, she just stared at the piano and pretended not to hear Brian's song!

"Hey, why don't we all play something together?" Naomi suggested during a lull in Brian's music. He stopped playing, suddenly aware of his audience.

"Uh, sure," he agreed. "What'll we play?"

Richard shuffled his feet and plucked at the lowest string on his instrument. It responded with a throaty *bommmmmm*. "How about something with a real strong beat? Let's get moving!"

Grandma shuddered but didn't disagree. "All right."

"Let's do 'Power in the Blood.'" Bruce suggested in a moment of bravery. "Everyone knows that."

To my amazement, this diverse crowd agreed to try it. Before I could pull out my own guitar, Grandma chose a key on the piano, and Richard started up his bass. Even Brian joined in.

As I gazed around the circle, I realized that I was viewing a special moment. How often do age, sex, worship style, and personality type all dim in a group's effort to accomplish something special? I watched as this collection of people each give a little bit in order to praise God with their music.

After that afternoon of music, I knew that praising God without offending others might not be as hard as I thought. If I retained an open mind and encouraged others to do the same, amazing things could happen. Instead of being appalled at a person's praise style, differing opinions might actually come together in a common goal!

There are virtually millions of ways to praise God. He is large enough to speak to me in millions of ways, so I must be able to give Him, the God I praise, a million expressions of my love as well.

Reference Points:

"Glorify the Lord with me; let us exalt his name together" (Psalm 34:3).

"Great is the Lord, and most worthy of praise, in the city of our

God, his holy mountain" (Psalm 48:1).

"The wild animals honor me, the jackals and the owls, because I provide water in the desert and streams in the wasteland, to give drink to my people, my chosen, the people I formed for myself that they may proclaim my praise" (Isaiah 43:20, 21).

"Because your love is better than life, my lips will glorify you. I will praise you as long as I live, and in your name I will lift up my hands" (Psalm 63:3, 4).

"Sing to him, sing praise to him; tell of all his wonderful acts. Glory in his holy name; let the hearts of those who seek the Lord rejoice. Look to the Lord and his strength; seek his face always" (1 Chronicles 16:9-11).

"'They will come and shout for joy on the heights of Zion; they will rejoice in the bounty of the Lord—the grain, the new wine and the oil, the young of the flocks and herds. They will be like a well-watered garden, and they will sorrow no more. Then maidens will dance and be glad, young men and old as well. I will turn their mourning into gladness; I will give them comfort and joy instead of sorrow. I will satisfy the priests with abundance, and my people will be filled with my bounty,' declares the Lord" (Jeremiah 31:12-14).

Chapter Thirty-five

God *Who Sends*

(Based on Jerimiah 1)

I tried that once. What you're doing, that is.

It was years ago. I was still young. Living by myself, except for the visions. I don't know what else to call them. I'd be fixing something up on my property, minding my own business, when all of a sudden I'd feel Him coming. Like a whirlwind, He overtook my soul. I dreaded it and longed for it all at once. I know that sounds strange, but I can't think of a better way to describe it. When He came over me, I couldn't help myself. I'd grab my staff and throw on my cloak and rush to the city, His spirit prodding me all the way.

Once I got there, it was always the same. I'd stand in the square and speak His words, words I hadn't planned or known before I uttered them. And did the people listen? Only rarely! Some of the arguing wives would stop and stare at me for a while. A few greasy merchants usually scowled at me for interrupting their business. Sometimes an earnest young man would listen intently. But even if there were no earnest young men to console me, I could never stop the torrent of words that He unleashed. Not for the world.

What did I tell them? Well, nothing I would want

Yahweh to direct at me! Usually I delivered messages of destruction and judgment. If He had a message, I communicated it. Simple as that.

In the beginning I felt honored by His desire to speak through me. But after the first several experiences as His delivery boy, I noticed a pattern: Jeremiah speaks for Yahweh; Jeremiah gets in trouble. It never failed. People simply don't like to hear the truth.

Well, I got tired of that routine pretty quickly. So the next time I felt Him coming on, I braced myself and kept right on picking burrs from my donkey's tail.

Oh, the pain of it! If I can say one thing for Yahweh, I can tell you that He is persistent. Do you know? The feeling grew and grew until I felt as though my very heart would explode with the importance of His message!

You're right. I did it. I grabbed my staff and threw on my cloak and rushed to the city—the same old story.

But you must know all about that. You get the feeling, don't you? You know, the feeling that you must do a certain thing for Yahweh? The knowledge that He has a job in mind just for you?

What? You get the feeling but you're afraid to speak or act? What are you afraid of? *Rejection*? Let me tell you something: I experienced *torture* for my obedience to Yahweh, and I still did what He commanded. What's a little rejection compared with the miracle of His plan, after all?

Yes, I too was afraid in the beginning. I was afraid to make myself look like a fool on the whim of a God I'd never seen. I cringed at the laughing, scorning eyes of my people. How could Yahweh ask me to do something so humiliating? I admit it freely—I was afraid.

But listen closely. I got over it real quick. Now when I stand to deliver a message that will endanger my life and my dignity, I have the courage to continue. I understand your fear of looking foolish for Yahweh. But you must understand my strength to obey anyway.

Do you want to know what gives me this courage? If I ignore the feeling, I must explain myself to its Sender. You see, Yahweh does not give impressions and directions for no reason at all. He has a purpose in mind for every impulse He sends to us. And when we ignore them on the basis of our own fear, we're blatantly disobeying Him. Now, I don't know about you, but I never want to disobey

Him. After all, Yahweh is my God, the God who sends. And I am honored to be His messenger.

Reference Points:

"If I say, 'I will not mention him or speak any more in his name,' his word is in my heart like a burning fire, shut up in my bones. I am weary of holding it in; indeed, I cannot" (Jeremiah 20:9).

"I heard the voice of the Lord saying, 'Whom shall I send? And who will go for us?' And I said, 'Here am I. Send me!'" (Isaiah 6:8).

"God's gifts and his call are irrevocable" (Romans 11:29).

"We cannot help speaking about what we have seen and heard" (Acts 4:20).

"The world and its desires pass away, but the man who does the will of God lives forever" (1 John 2:17).

Chapter Thirty-six

God *of the Vibrant*

(Based on Acts 6 and 7)

"Aren't you a Jew?" The man's face shoves into my field of vision.

"Yes," I answer slowly. "Yes, I am a Jew." My honesty will cost me.

He sneers at me. "I don't believe it. No self-respecting Jew could preach such blasphemy."

"I preach only the truth of my risen Saviour, Jesus Christ."

"Risen Saviour? *Risen Saviour?"* the man explodes. Heads turn in our direction and shuffling feet still to silence. "This man speaks of a risen Saviour!" Sensing his audience, the man shouts louder. "You—you slithering pretense of a Jew, go straight back where you came from—to Hades!" my sweating antagonist yells.

I square my shoulders and turn away. Only months before, these Jews had shouted my name in the streets. *Saul, Saul!* they screamed. *This is Saul who purges our race. Saul, Saul!*

As I walk through the crowd, I sigh again. I am no longer "Saul, Saul." Now my few friends know me as "Paul. Paul, the man Jesus touched." I've come a long way in the past few months. Ever since that day on the road to Damascus I've seen in a different light.

Well, no. I can't say it started that day. I suppose it all began on the day they stoned the young man, Stephen. Stephen was my worst enemy, even after his death. *I'll kill him,* I'd promised myself as I paced the synagogue floor. *I'll hunt him down and kill him for his belief in Jesus Christ.*

Naturally, Stephen was a prime target for my anti-Jesus campaign. Stephen, with the loosely curling hair and athletic stature. Stephen, with the fearless strong voice and the talent for attracting crowds of listeners to his every uttered syllable. Stephen, with those ghastly penetrating eyes.

I first met his gaze when I faced him in the Sanhedrin council that would decide his fate. He stood alone before us all, a slight figure beside the crisp-robed Pharisees, awaiting their verdict with perfect composure.

Shake, man! I silently commanded. *Tremble and cry and beg for mercy. Fall to your knees and admit your guilt. And for the love of the one true God, lower your eyes like the criminal you are.*

But this impudent man in the thin gray robe did not lower his gaze. Instead, he assessed the crowd as though *we* were the ones on trial. I'd spent the past year chasing this criminal around the country, and he had the gall to stare me in the face!

I took a step backward when our eyes finally locked, and unwittingly stepped on a Pharisee's toes. I was too busy wondering what I saw in those unblinking brown eyes. Of course, I never found out. At just that moment the leader of the Sanhedrin stood to proclaim his judgment.

"We find you guilty!" he boomed. "Guilty of blasphemy and lies and a thousand other offenses against the Most High God."

But even that didn't break Stephen's composure. He turned slowly away from me and searched the crowd once more. "Look," he suddenly exclaimed, staring at the ceiling. *"Look! I see Heaven! And I see Jesus, the Son of Man, standing beside His Father, God."*

Suddenly all semblance of peace vanished. The crowd grew vicious as they ripped and clawed and jerked their captive toward the Stoning Ground.

I didn't help them with the stoning. After all my efforts to secure this vagabond, I didn't throw even one rock. Instead, I let the crowd pile their coats at my feet. And I watched as Stephen's living eyes glazed and dulled and finally closed forever.

Living? Yes, I believe they were. For even after he died Stephen's gaze continued to haunt me. I sought it everywhere, this intense peace he had *looked* into my soul. I searched the faces of my partners in persecution and found nothing. I met the gaze of servants, foreigners, and Gentiles. Each face revealed nothing more than a bland acceptance of life, religion, and country.

But I couldn't stand that blandness again. Not after Stephen's relentless gaze. Oh, I pretended everything was normal. I think I even believed myself. But deep inside, from the moment I met his gaze, I knew I lacked something that Stephen possessed. Something I desperately wanted to experience.

Not until that day on the Damascus road did I realize that my missing ingredient was God, whose very Son I had denied again and again. Not until my own eyes were blinded with the light and the power of His presence. Like a fool, I asked Him, "Who are You, Lord?" I'd spoken His name with my own lips and not recognized it.

"Swine!" The parting call of the angry man reaches me halfway down the street. A thousand biting insults spring to mind, and I know I can give him the tongue-lashing he deserves. I turn to face him as he stands in the shadow of a moldy wall.

I don't speak. Instead, I follow Stephen's example, and Christ's before that. I merely look at this frustrated man, whose black hair now hangs in clumps across his glistening forehead. He stares back for a moment, and I think I've given him the message correctly. Then he whirls around and disappears into a shadowy doorway.

What did I tell him? I said, *I love you. I love you, although hate comes much easier. I love you because I love Jesus and because Jesus loves me. I want you to know my joy. I want you to be as free as I am. And I'll always love you.*

I'm not sure he understood. Most people turn away and try to forget our shared moment. But I'm glad God reminded me of Stephen's eyes today. Eyes that held peace, strength, and a quality of existence that can be found only in deep communion with God. A resilience and a joy that one word explains: vibrance.

Yes, I saw vibrance in Stephen's eyes that day. And I pray I showed that vibrance to the man on the street. A vibrance that resonates in every pore of my life. A joy anyone can find when they accept its source—God, the God of the vibrant.

Reference Points:

"You are the light of the world. A city on a hill cannot be hidden. Neither do people light a lamp and put it under a bowl. Instead they put it on its stand, and it gives light to everyone in the house. In the same way, let your light shine before men, that they may see your good deeds and praise your Father in heaven" (Matthew 5:14-16).

"All who were sitting in the Sanhedrin looked intently at Stephen, and they saw that his face was like the face of an angel" (Acts 6:15).

"When Moses came down from Mount Sinai with the two tablets of the Testimony in his hands, he was not aware that his face was radiant because he had spoken with the Lord" (Exodus 34:29).

"Those who are wise will shine like the brightness of the heavens, and those who lead many to righteousness, like the stars for ever and ever" (Daniel 12:3).

Chapter Thirty-seven

God *of the Useless*

A young girl hurries down the hard-packed path toward home. Her clear brown eyes focus only on each step in front of her. Though the village is alive with color and sound, she notices only the worn toe straps of her sandals, following her toes down the road.

"Watch out!"

Suddenly the cry of a small boy breaks her reverie. Just in time, she swerves to avoid hitting him. She laughs when she sees his burden—a water jug at least as tall as he is.

"Can I help you?" she offers, bending down to his height.

He lifts his chin higher and puffs out his chest. "No," he responds gruffly. "I can do it myself." With a superhuman heave, he hoists the jar onto his shoulder and plods on down the path.

Mary smiles shakily at his retreating figure and wipes her eyes with a trembling hand. *It's always the same, isn't it? Nobody ever needs my help.* Passing a food-fragrant doorway, she remembers. *Mother never wanted my help in the kitchen. Father was too busy to need me. And my older brothers? No more could I help them than a chicken could pull a donkey's load!*

"Hello, Mary." Another voice interrupts her thoughts.

"Good afternoon, Hilda. A fine day for walking, isn't it?"

The graying woman sighs and swipes at her broad sweating forehead. "If you've got time to walk, it is. I've been helping my Jonas in the shop all afternoon! Oh, those customers! They make me want to scream! Always needing attention, they are!" She pauses to stare at the girl's solemn face. "Don't look so glum, child! Every marriage isn't as tedious as mine! Just think—you will have such a nice quiet life with Joseph. No respectable woman could help him in the shop." She wipes her hands on her ample brown robe and chortles to herself. "I'll envy your leisure, little Mary."

Mary turns before Hilda can see the sob in her eyes. *And I envy your business, my friend. More than you will ever know.*

Hurrying through the village, Mary prays for no more encounters with humanity. *Just some time to think, God. That's all I want.* She ducks past Joseph's open carpenter's shop, hoping he hasn't recognized her profile. A stray dog slinks through an alley, and she frowns at its scrawny form. *I feel just like that dog. No identity, no talents, and no shining future. Where, God? Where is my place in this world? What can I do for You?*

"Almost there?"

Joseph nods, his week-old beard highlighted in the setting sun. "Just over the next hill."

You said that 12 hills ago, Mary sighs silently. *I want to rest. I want to sleep. I want a warm dry place for the Baby. I want to keep Him safe.*

The Baby. Mary's step lightens as she remembers the precious load within her. Could it be only months ago that the strange white being filled her room with his presence? Could it be that just months ago she sat trembling before his strange greeting?

Greetings, you who are highly favored! The Lord is with you! Before she could scream, the being had continued. *Do not be afraid. God is with you. You're going to have a baby Boy and name Him Jesus. This Baby will save the world from its awful sins. He is the Son of God.*

And then, as though it were the most normal thing in the world to discuss her pregnancy with a strange glowing intruder, she'd asked him questions. *How do you know? How can this be? What does it mean? Why?*

He'd gently reminded her that God can do all things. There, standing in a dusty cottage on the outskirts of a long-forgotten village, the angel had spoken with her as freely as a friend.

And as she listened, Mary finally knew. She knew that all the talent and riches and personality in the world could never take the place of what she had to offer. She knew that beyond high dreams and bright prospects her future loomed vast and important. She knew that for the first time in her life she was needed by Someone more powerful than Mother or Father or even Joseph could ever be.

I am the Lord's servant, she'd told the angel calmly. *Let this thing come to pass.*

And he was gone. Alone again, Mary was forced to explain her expanding abdomen to a suspicious world. But her final words to the angel echoed in her mind and gave her courage for the onslaught of gossip that followed. *I am the Lord's servant.*

Back on the rocky trail to Bethlehem, Mary smiles at Joseph's back. The news had nearly split them apart. But in the end he consented to share his wife with the forces at work in heaven. And he accepted her simple explanation in silence. *I am the Lord's servant.*

In three steps they crest the final hill. Below them the lights of Bethlehem twinkle like misplaced stars on a shadowy landscape. Mary's aching body protests at the thought of another jarring downhill trek, but she straightens her shoulders and smiles resolutely.

Beside her, Joseph smiles too, and Mary starts down the hill with a song in her soul. *It doesn't matter if nobody thinks I'm important,* she decides happily. *I know that I'm completely priceless to the God whose Son I carry, my God who turns the useless into irreplaceable treasures in His sight.*

Reference Points:

"He said to me, 'My grace is sufficient for you, for my power is made perfect in weakness.' Therefore I will boast all the more gladly about my weaknesses, so that Christ's power may rest on me. That is why, for Christ's sake, I delight in weaknesses, in insults, in hard-

ships, in persecutions, in difficulties. For when I am weak, then I am strong" (2 Corinthians 12:9, 10).

"Whoever wants to become great among you must be your servant, and whoever wants to be first must be slave of all. For even the Son of Man did not come to be served, but to serve, and to give his life as a ransom for many" (Mark 10:43-45).

"Don't let anyone look down on you because you are young, but set an example for the believers in speech, in life, in love, in faith and in purity" (1 Timothy 4:12).

"Sitting down, Jesus called the Twelve and said, 'If anyone wants to be first, he must be the very last, and the servant of all'" (Mark 9:35).

"The greatest among you will be your servant. For whoever exalts himself will be humbled, and whoever humbles himself will be exalted" (Matthew 23:11, 12).

Chapter Thirty-eight

God *Who Comes*

(Based on Mark 14:32-38; John 20:24-28)

Morning.

I can tell by the slightly less-black slits between my window bars that the sun is on the rise. Outside a faraway bird begins to sing. Perhaps he sees the sun already. I swallow and roll over to face the wall. *Just another hour of sleep.*

I'm back in Gethsemane again. Instantly I recognize Peter's profile in the shadows. James sits farther off, staring toward the spot where the Master departed.

"What's wrong with Jesus?" he asks, worry lines creasing his forehead.

"I don't know," Peter growls. "But I'm gettin' mighty tired. How about a little sleep?" He pillows his head on a nearby clump of grass and closes his eyes.

"Peter!" James sounds like an angry mother, and I can't help smiling. "Peter, the Master asked us to watch and pray. If you're going to close your eyes, at least keep praying for Him!"

Peter sighs noisily. "I'm praying; I'm praying!" Within minutes, his breathing slows and deepens to a noisy wheeze.

"He's found us sleeping once tonight," James fusses. "We can't let it happen again. How will we ever be first in His kingdom if—"

"Forget about the kingdom!" I snap. "We ruined

our chances for that a long time ago. Besides, the Master loves us. He knows we're tired. I'm sure He won't mind if we relax for a few minutes before we pray."

"I don't know . . ." James peers into the gloom around us. "He said—"

"C'mon, brother." I pat the ground beside me. "You're tired. I'll wake you up in a few minutes, and then we'll pray."

"All right," he finally agrees. "Just a few more minutes. Jesus sure was right. The spirit is willing but, oh, the flesh is so weak!"

And then I hear Jesus' urgent voice above us. "Still sleeping? Look around you! This is the hour of My death!"

Suddenly I'm wide awake on my mat, back in the chilly room I inhabit. I stare at the wall, inches from my nose, and trace its dark brown crevices with my eyes. I, John, slept while my Master suffered in the garden. Would He have lived if I had stayed awake?

My mind reeling with tormenting questions, I stumble to my feet and face the window. The strips of light are brighter now, and I can see shadows of the world outside. Am I really in prison? The cold roundness of those bars against my face affirms it. But can it be? Only a year ago I sat mourning His death in the upper room. My palms tingle against the bars I grasp so tightly.

"Look at My palms, Thomas." His command is so silent it can easily be ignored, yet so direct every man in the room looks as well.

A gasp escapes Thomas's lips, and he cringes away from the wounds we all see.

"Do you believe?" Jesus asks him. "Now do you believe that I am your Master? Here, Thomas. Come here and feel My side. A sword punctured there."

Thomas approaches and feels the wounded side. Now he stands as one condemned before his judge.

"My Lord," he confesses softly, his chest heaving with unacknowledged sobs. "My Lord and my God." The expression in his eyes speaks the words his soul cannot. How could he doubt his Master's sacrifice? How could he doubt His power to live? How could he doubt His proven identity?

I look at my feet and notice that I'm shuffling. I doubted Him too. I wondered if I'd ever see the Master again. I felt the finality of

His last ragged breath. I demeaned His capabilities with my lack of belief. I refused to trust Him at His unbreakable word.

A twig snaps from a tree and one drab leaf minces to the earth. I move away from the window and lean against the opposite wall. Almost overnight the seasons have begun to change. I can't imagine spending the cold season locked in this mud-brick cage without a fire. The glamour of suffering for Jesus is losing its appeal, and I long for warmth and fresh bedding.

At least I have my pen. I scan the words I must have written last night. I remember the dream as vividly as Gethsemane, but reading the words still excites a strange thrill in my heart.

Behold, I am coming soon. I remember writing the ideas as fast as my vision supplied them. *My reward is with Me, and I will give to everyone according to what he has done. I am the Alpha and the Omega, the First and the Last, the Beginning and the End. . . . Yes, I am coming soon!*

I shudder and turn from the page. *What have I done? What have I done, Master, that You should give me anything?* My mind replays a thousand tiny scenes, and I see my weakness and doubt in sharp contrast to His strength. *You gave me nothing but confirmation of Your power, Jesus, yet I continually let You down and doubted You. Yes, what have I done to deserve anything from You?*

A gust of wind pushes through my window and circles the room. Again I remember that the seasons are changing.

And then I have it. Standing alone in this ugly room, I know what I must do. I realize that I can still show the Master my love. "I haven't deserted You yet," I mumble, reaching for my instrument again. "I know You better than I did, and I know You'll keep Your word. Every promise You make is as unstoppable as the changing seasons. I can only believe and prepare for what I know to be inevitable. And I will."

Suddenly I'm filled with a sense of urgency. It could happen any minute now! In several quick strokes I add a few words to the messy notes I wrote last night. Satisfied, I set down the pen and regard my work. The words speak more clearly than a five-page testimony ever could. They tell Him plain as bright day that I believe and am on His side forever. They speak from my finally peaceful heart.

The morning bird sings again, and I jerk my head toward the window. The sun seems inexplicably bright, and I rush forward. Could it be? Could He be fulfilling His promise right now? Smiling like a fool for Him, I clasp those bars again and stand ready for the moment I know will come. Beside me another stray breeze ruffles several word-filled pages on the table. At the bottom of one, four words stand out in freshly written ink. But I've forgotten them in my excitement, and they sit unnoticed on the table while I scan the sky above.

Amen. Come, Lord Jesus.

Reference Points:

"'Yes, it is as you say,' Jesus replied. 'But I say to all of you: In the future you will see the Son of Man sitting at the right hand of the Mighty One and coming on the clouds of heaven'" (Matthew 26:64).

"Be self-controlled and alert. Your enemy the devil prowls around like a roaring lion looking for someone to devour. Resist him, standing firm in the faith, because you know that your brothers throughout the world are undergoing the same kind of sufferings. And the God of all grace, who called you to his eternal glory in Christ, after you have suffered a little while, will himself restore you and make you strong, firm and steadfast" (1 Peter 5:8-10).

"You know very well that the day of the Lord will come like a thief in the night" (1 Thessalonians 5:2).

"No one knows about that day or hour, not even the angels in heaven, nor the Son, but only the Father. Be on guard! Be alert ! You do not know when that time will come" (Mark 13:32, 33).

Chapter Thirty-nine

God *Who Saves*

"Help! Somebody help me!" A thin high voice grabs my attention. My head jerks up and I see a crowd of my friends standing, paralyzed, on the opposite shore.

"Help!" Again, that frantic cry. "Help me!" From the corner of my eye I watch as Brandon's head disappears under the black water of Okanogan River.

Do something! my brain commands. Before I can plan it, I'm striding through the water toward him. "Brandon!" I call. "Brandon, come over here!"

His frantic eyes catch my gaze for a minute. I'm running now, but the water holds me back like hardening cement. The river washes around my neck and lifts the hair from my back. *Getting deeper . . .*

"Brandon!" He surfaces again, closer than I thought. "Reach out and grab my hand!" My feet barely touch the bottom, but I strain toward his flailing arms anyway. We're still too far. I forsake my last foothold to reach his hand. "Hold on!" I order, treading water with my one free arm. *Where's the bottom?* My feet reach down into cold wetness and find no firm ground.

My instructions are useless. Brandon grabs my hand and claws further up my arm. "Help!" he screams again, choking on a sudden wash of water. "Help me!"

"I am!" I pant. Suddenly Brandon grows unbearably heavy and I realize that he's clinging to my shoulder, nearly pushing me underwater. "Let go of my hair!"

Irrational by now, Brandon grabs my long pony tail and maneuvers onto my back. Now we're both struggling in the water, and somehow he's become my enemy.

"Stop that!" I shout just before he scrambles up my back and onto my shoulders. Without warning I enter a silent dark underworld. Above me Brandon kicks and claws for another breath of air. His panic seeps into my mind as well.

I can't breathe! I push and shove and scream into the earless water, but no one hears my cries. Just when I know I'm going to die, I shoot to the surface and snatch a ragged breath of air before he grabs me again. Somehow we both stay on the surface this time, our legs and arms churning the water to an angry foam. *Got . . . to . . . save . . . Brandon!* I think doggedly as he yanks my head backward with a jerk to my ponytail. But he won't let me!

We're sinking, sinking—and I know we will die. As I submerge for the last time, I see a bright blur to my left. *Light. Sunshine. "AIR!*

Suddenly I pop to the surface again. No weight holds me down. In fact, I see Brandon speeding off toward shore in the arms of my teacher, Mr. Kyle. Dazed and too tired to move, I let the current wash me ashore a few yards downstream.

"Are you all right?" Mr. Kyle touches my shoulder, and I look up into his dripping face. Droplets of water sparkle in his red hair. A flock of goosebumps form on each arm. Behind us, Brandon coughs up another mouthful of water.

"I'm alive." I nod and struggle to my feet. "I'm alive."

Alive. I'm so grateful for this fact that I forget to thank Mr. Kyle. Not until I'm dry and warm and finally stop shaking do I remember. Brandon and I survived our fight with the river solely because Mr. Kyle saved our lives. I couldn't rescue Brandon alone. And in the end, I couldn't even rescue myself.

Telling this story still makes me shudder. I remember with brutal clarity the churning water, the clawing hands, and the screaming lungs. And now, along with my memory of the rescue, come other pictures as well.

I'll help you, I promise a sobbing friend. *I'm sure we can figure something out to make your life a little better.* But nothing solves her problems. Within weeks we're both caught in a web of confusion and pain.

But he's my friend! I protest when someone suggests I'm too involved with someone's troubles. *I have to be there for him. Besides, who else can he turn to?* But when we're both discouraged and alone with the pain, I see my friend's wisdom.

You'll be just fine, I comfort a frustrated family member. *Come talk to me whenever you need to.* Eventually, though, the stress becomes too much for either of us to handle and ends in an explosion of anger.

Even though I want to solve every problem, I lose every battle I fight without God. Time and again I learn this lesson. But still I persist in trying to rescue those I love. I simply can't do it. I've failed enough to know that for sure. But I know Someone who won't fail. Someone who, like Mr. Kyle, shows up whenever I scream "Help." Someone who knows how to handle the situations that pull me under. Someone who loves me enough to fight (and win) the battles I'd surely lose alone.

Who is He? I'm sure you know Him. He is God, the God who saves me and you and an entire world of drowning people.

Reference Points:

"The Lord is my strength and my song; he has become my salvation. Shouts of joy and victory resound in the tents of the righteous: 'The Lord's right hand has done mighty things! The Lord's right hand is lifted high; the Lord's right hand has done mighty things!' I will not die but live, and will proclaim what the Lord has done" (Psalm 118:14-17).

"The disciples went and woke him, saying, 'Lord, save us! We're going to drown!' He replied, 'You of little faith, why are you so afraid?' Then he got up and rebuked the winds and the waves, and it was completely calm" (Matthew 8:25, 26).

"Come to me, all you who are weary and burdened, and I will

give you rest. Take my yoke upon you and learn from me, for I am gentle and humble in heart, and you will find rest for your souls. For my yoke is easy and my burden is light" (Matthew 11:28-30).

"I can do everything through him who gives me strength" (Philippians 4:13).

"He gives strength to the weary and increases the power of the weak. Even youths grow tired and weary, and young men stumble and fall; but those who hope in the Lord will renew their strength. They will soar on wings like eagles; they will run and not grow weary, they will walk and not be faint" (Isaiah 40:29-31).

"But when he saw the wind, he was afraid and, beginning to sink, cried out, 'Lord, save me!' Immediately Jesus reached out his hand and caught him" (Matthew 14:30, 31).

Chapter Forty

God *I Surrender To*

The blue light stares intently into my dilated right pupil.

"Hold still, hold still," Dr. Snow cautions from somewhere behind a big black machine.

I grit my teeth and stare straight ahead.

Several eternities later Dr. Snow swings the pressure-reading device away from my face. My world looks as blurry as a foggy tropical morning, but I smile in the direction of his fuzzy face.

"Does everything look all right?"

"No." Dr. Snow's tone makes me catch my breath.

"What's wrong? What's wrong with my eye?"

He bends over his machine and rechecks the results. "These pressure readings are far too high. They're in the glaucoma range. Yes, you definitely have glaucoma."

I squeeze the fingers of my left hand so tightly that I can feel the contour of each bone. "Wh-what did you say?"

"Glaucoma. You have it. If I were you, I'd think twice about being a missionary."

My already blurry world begins to reel. "Can—can you tell me a little more about glaucoma?"

The next half hour of medical terms flies completely over my head. While Dr. Snow explains and reexplains my condition, my mind scrambles for answers of its own. *Think twice about being a missionary? He doesn't want me to go; wants me close to medical attention.*

"So what can I do about it?" I finally blurt into a professionally polite silence.

He sighs and snaps his clipboard shut. "Nothing but wait."

Nothing.

As I stare out the car window on the way home, I realize that I haven't done "nothing" for a very long time. I spent my sophomore year in college working three jobs, taking 18 credits a quarter, and taxing my capabilities to the limit. Amid all the bustle, however, I managed to plan in a year as a student missionary with my roommate, Angie. *It will be fun,* I told myself. *And I'll be doing God's work.*

But when school got out and summer began, I wasn't sure I had made the right choice. I felt queasy about disappearing into the jungle for a year, but I knew I couldn't back out. So I halfheartedly planned and counted off the days until I'd vanish into the wilds of Nepal. Two months . . . One month . . . Three weeks . . .

And now I've got glaucoma. I press my nose against the already smudged window and watch yellow fields ripple by. *God, what should I do now?*

Nothing.

His answer comes as clearly as Dr. Snow's recent declaration. Mentally, I shuffle my feet and check my watch. *You've got to be kidding, God! I'm giving this year of my life to You, and You want me to do nothing? For how long?*

I receive no reply. As the weeks tick by, I wonder if "nothing" will become my permanent career.

"All right, God," I mumble one morning during worship. "All right, You win."

Silence. Several birds outside trill to each other and fly away.

"God, I can't take it any longer. I've done nothing for so long that I'm willing to do *anything!* I'll work in a garbage dump if You want me to. I'll go to Nepal, in spite of my eye. I'll even clean a zoo! Whatever You want is exactly what I want . . . I promise."

I sigh and close my Bible. Still the silence persists, but I'm used to it now. Today's prayer doesn't seem earth-shattering, but I know it's a step in the right direction. As I snap on my computer screen and prepare for another day of writing, I smile at a mental picture of me cleaning a zoo for God. *Yep, I'll even do that.*

"Hello?" I answer the phone several hours later.

"Hi, Sarah," a friendly voice on the line responds. "Do you have any plans for the next several weeks?"

I grin. "I'm doing absolutely nothing! Why?"

This phone call from a complete stranger begins a long chain of miraculous events. By the time the dust settles, I live on the other side of the nation, working at exactly the job God had planned for me: recruiting my peers to be missionaries overseas.

I love my job. I know I'm exactly where God wants me. And finally, after years of tedious planning and disappointments, I know how to find this assurance. I must forget my own wishes in the overwhelming desire to find God's will. I must give every lingering detail directly into the nail-scarred hands of God. And I must leave my life within His care. In short, I must surrender everything to this God I'm learning to rely on.

Reference Points:

"I desire to do your will, O my God; your law is within my heart" (Psalm 40:8).

"Father, if you are willing, take this cup from me; yet not my will, but yours be done" (Luke 22:42).

"Whatever you ask for in prayer, believe that you have received it, and it will be yours" (Mark 11:24).

"For the sake of your servant and according to your will, you have done this great thing and made known all these great promises. There is no one like you, O Lord, and there is no God but you, as we have heard with our own ears" (1 Chronicles 17:19, 20).

Chapter Forty-one

God *My Priority*

"Sarah."

Mom's curt voice sounds hazily in my 10-year-old brain. Carefully I adjust the dress on my Cabbage Patch doll and hold her up for inspection.

"Sarah."

Again that persistent call.

"Sarah, where are you?"

Suddenly the bedroom door bursts open, and Mom swoops in like a disoriented tornado.

"Right here," I reply absently, adjusting the terrycloth strap on my summer tank top. "What do you want?" I notice that sweat has beaded on Mom's forehead like condensation on a glass of ice water. She swipes a hand across her face and the droplets disappear.

"Sarah, will you listen to me very closely?"

I nod.

She walks jerkily toward her bed, where I've been playing with my doll, and sits down beside me. "Do you remember the fire that started several days ago?"

Again, I nod. "What about it?"

"Well, the fire department just called. It's getting close to our home, and they told us we have to evacuate." Her choppy words chase themselves straight into my heart.

"We're leaving?" I screech. "But what about the animals? What about the garden? Will everything burn up?" I visualize ravenous flames devouring every inch of our property. "What about my doll?"

Mom sighs and stares up at the ceiling. Just then Charley tromps into the room with two wooden apple crates. "Here they are, Mom."

"Thank you."

I glance at his face and know instantly that Mom has told him already. She stands and hands me a box. "Here, Sarah. You and Charley take these and fill them with your most important things. I'm sorry, but this is all we'll have room for. All right?"

We nod in silence and shuffle toward the door.

"And kids—whatever you do, please hurry!"

I walk to my room and switch on the light. My blue-checkered bedspread and matching curtains seem somehow ugly today. My dolls and stuffed animals leer at the choice I have to make. *Go ahead,* they dare me. *Leave one of us behind. You won't be able to sleep, knowing you let us burn to death. Go right ahead!*

I gulp and set my white windup teddy bear in the bottom of the box. "What should I take?" I mumble, surveying the room one more time. Precious books and pictures scream from every shelf for salvation. Already I know I'll fit only a fraction of my treasures into the box at my feet. Sighing, I try once again to rank my possessions in order of importance and reach for another stuffed animal.

Several minutes later Charley and I emerge from our rooms and stand facing each other in the hallway. "What did you bring?" he asks.

"Not much." I gesture toward my loaded box. Inside, a pile of coloring books and a box of crayons sigh in relief. Several of my choicest stuffed animals stare smugly at each other. And one or two books top the pile. Charley's box holds matchbox cars, various mechanical treasures, and a few family pictures. We nod at each other, shy in this sudden crisis.

Mom bustles down the hall, a pile of clothes in her arms. "Are you ready?"

"Uh, yeah." I mumble.

"All right, just put the boxes in the living room, and I'll take care of them." Her voice is as tight as a brand-new window screen, and I wonder exactly where Dad's at right now. "Charley, can you help me—"

"Wait!" Just as Charley bends to pick up my box, I dash back into my room and return with a small burgundy book. "I forgot something."

Gingerly, I balance it atop my pile of belongings and read the title to myself. *Holy Bible.* Almost imperceptibly Charley nods toward his own black Bible, propped neatly against one side of the box. Together we hoist our most precious possessions and carry them to the living room. *We'll never see this house again,* I think soberly. *This box holds my only memories of home.*

Miraculously, the fire burns a clean-cut horseshoe around the shape of our family property. While the men fight the flames, the women pray and watch the children. And at the end of that long, long battle, we reclaim our home in the country, unscathed by any flames.

Carefully, I unpack my box and replace each item in its rightful spot. I return the Bible to its dusty shelf, where it sits unused for the next several months. And though I'm only 10, I wonder, *Why did I bring this Bible, anyway? What really matters in my life?*

"Sarah, I've figured out what really matters in my life." Ten years later Charley's sudden comment is an echo from my past.

I hold the phone receiver a little closer. "What?"

"Well"—his voice sounds closer than 2,000 miles away as he continues—"I've been camping alone for the past week, and I had plenty of time to think."

"What did you learn?" I demand impatiently.

He chuckles. "I learned that nothing matters, Sarah. College doesn't matter. A job doesn't matter. Money doesn't matter. My hobbies don't matter. None of the things I live for—music, backpacking, computers—matter."

"So?"

"What really matters is the people I know and how I treat them. I can't take anything with me from this world except my love for people and my love for God."

I allow a respectful moment of silence before commenting. "Wow. Maybe I should go camping alone too!"

Once again Charley reminds me of something so important I haven't seen it for myself. He reminds me that, like the Bible I halfheartedly tossed on my pile of possessions, outward appearances won't save me in the end. Even if I go to church every day until I'm 90, I won't have what really matters—unless I make it first in my heart today.

What matters the most? I finally know. Now it's up to me to decide: Will I make God my priority?

Reference Points:

"Love the Lord your God with all your heart and with all your soul and with all your strength" (Deuteronomy 6:5).

"You shall have no other gods before me" (Exodus 20:3).

"Do not worry about your life, what you will eat or drink; or about your body, what you will wear. Is not life more important than food, and the body more important than clothes? Look at the birds of the air; they do not sow or reap or store away in barns, and yet your heavenly Father feeds them. Are you not much more valuable than they? Who of you by worrying can add a single hour to his life? And why do you worry about clothes? See how the lilies of the field grow. They do not labor or spin. Yet I tell you that not even Solomon in all his splendor was dressed like one of these. If that is how God clothes the grass of the field, which is here today and tomorrow is thrown into the fire, will he not much more clothe you, O you of little faith? So do not worry, saying, 'What shall we eat?' or 'What shall we drink?' or 'What shall we wear?' For the pagans run after all these things, and your heavenly Father knows that you need them. But seek first his kingdom and his righteousness, and all these things will be given to you as well" (Matthew 6:25-33).

"Jesus said to him, 'Away from me, Satan! For it is written: "Worship the Lord your God, and serve him only"'" (Matthew 4:10).

Chapter Forty-two

God I Experience

"Sarah, look!" Mom whispers from the left side of her mouth.

"What?" I whisper back without moving my face.

"On the rostrum." Mom clamps her lips together and smoothes her dress—the perfect Sabbath-morning mother once again.

Beside her, I strain to see the bright-orange rostrum. In the foreground Pastor Fleming sways from side to side, emphasizing each point by leaning a new direction. That's not very unusual.

Behind him a stoic row of elders stares intently at the back wall of the church. Occasionally Bruce recrosses his legs, and I know he's anticipating his wife's home-cooked dinner.

Beside Bruce, Lloyd furrows his white eyebrows and wrinkles his forehead in concentration. I wonder if he's trying to read the pastor's notes.

And on the far left, Grandpa sits as calmly as an eagle on a cliff. *What does Mom see?* I ask myself.

And then I spot it: the tip of Grandpa's left ear wiggles ever so slightly. *Is he having a left-ear stroke?* I wonder. Before I can panic, his right earlobe wiggles in response. And while I'm still processing that unexpected movement, both ears start to wiggle at once.

Beneath his slicked-back hair they resemble the ponderous wings of a Monarch butterfly.

I smother a guffaw. Mom jabs her foot into my calf for silence. Pastor Fleming talks on, oblivious to our unholy humor.

"Look, Mom," I whisper, turning slightly toward her. But I can't safely finish my sentence. Mom's ears, unmistakably similar to her father's, rise and fall like the only two leaves left on an autumn-smitten tree.

What has become of my family? I wonder during the remainder of our church service. *And how can I learn that incredible talent?*

"It's simple," Mom tells me on our way home. The wind blows through our open windows and ruffles her long blond hair. "Just think 'wiggle,' and they'll wiggle."

Wiggle, I think laboriously. *Wiggle. Wiggle.*

"They're not moving," Charley announces beside me, his own ears flapping like a tent in a windstorm. "You're not concentrating hard enough."

"I am too!" I wail. "I just can't get it! Mom, how did you learn?"

She laughs. "How did I learn? I remember the day it happened. I was in third grade, sitting in class, and all of a sudden my ears just started to wiggle."

"No way! Tell the truth!" I challenge, hitting the back of her headrest.

"I am. That's exactly how I learned to do it." Mom settles down and gives her ears a flippant toss. "You'll understand when you learn how."

Thanks, I grumble to myself. *Thanks for nothing.*

For the next several years I pester my family with persistent questions. "Dad, can you do it?" "Does it help to yawn first?" "So what if my whole scalp is moving—at least my ears are too!" "What do you mean, 'Think about smiling'? How's that supposed to help?"

But nothing unravels the ear-wiggling mystery. Until one day . . .

"Hey, look!" I grab Chris's arm and point to Melanie's head. "They're wiggling!"

In the front seat, Charley and Melanie burst into laughter. "Didn't you know I could move my ears?" his girlfriend wonders.

I lean forward. "Can you show me how?"

"Here we go again," Charley groans. But I'm oblivious to his sarcasm as Melanie explains each step of the process in careful detail.

"It's no use," I decide after 15 minutes of practice. "I'll give myself a headache trying to move them! I give up."

"Sarah!" Chris reaches out and turns my head sideways. "They're wiggling!"

"They are?" I repeat the expression I've just made. *"That's* what it feels like?"

"Yeah. Wow, they're actually moving!" Melanie grins and turns back toward the highway, but I feel like throwing a party.

"I'm finally wiggling my ears!"

Now the entire concept makes as much sense to me as it did to Mom in third grade. *Just think "wiggle" and they'll wiggle.* Her advice finally works! *You'll understand when you learn how.* More of Mom's wisdom sifts through my memory. As much as I'd longed for that peculiar family talent, I couldn't comprehend it until I experienced it myself. Until then ear-wiggling was as foreign and alluring as a vacation in Jamaica: simply beyond my comprehension.

"What does total peace feel like?" The question, uttered first when I was a small child, has always haunted my mind. Even then, I wanted something to still the unrest in my heart. At age 10 I often awoke in the night, knelt by my bed, and begged the Holy Spirit to give me His peace.

"I want to be happy," I sobbed into my pillow. "Please make me Your child." And sometimes a fleeting but soul-deep peace would flood my mind.

Finally I realized the truth. In order to attain and share God's peace, I must return to the mental state I experienced when I felt it first. Jesus says, "I tell you the truth, we speak of what we know, and we testify to what we have seen, but still you people do not accept our testimony" (John 3:11). No person can speak convincingly about God's peace without experiencing it for themselves. And no person can understand that peace until they know what it's like. "For the message of the cross is foolishness to those who are perishing, but to us who are being saved it is the power of God" (1 Corinthians 1:18).

They say knowing God is like riding a bike—once you've found Him, you know how to find Him again. But there are standard instructions for every new bike rider to follow: sit on the seat, push the pedals, hold the handlebars, and don't go too slowly.

I have my own theory: knowing God is more similar to wiggling your ears. It takes a different moment to trigger each person's discovery, but once you understand the concept, it makes perfect sense.

I like that analogy. I like the fact that my God is creative enough to let me discover Him in the way that works for me. *You'll understand when you learn how,* my mother once told me. And I have to agree. When I found Him for the first time, the joy of that discovery kept me searching for the same feeling again. I cannot live without Him now, not after I've felt His power. I cannot ignore the God who invites me to experience Him so deeply. Can you?

Reference Points:

"Taste and see that the Lord is good; blessed is the man who takes refuge in him" (Psalm 34:8).

"As the deer pants for streams of water, so my soul pants for you, O God. My soul thirsts for God, for the living God. When can I go and meet with God? My tears have been my food day and night, while men say to me all day long, 'Where is your God?' These things I remember as I pour out my soul: how I used to go with the multitude, leading the procession to the house of God, with shouts of joy and thanksgiving among the festive throng. Why are you downcast, O my soul? Why so disturbed within me? Put your hope in God, for I will yet praise him, my Savior and my God" (Psalm 42:1-5).

"I know whom I have believed, and am convinced that he is able to guard what I have entrusted to him for that day" (2 Timothy 1:12).

"One thing I ask of the Lord, this is what I seek: that I may dwell in the house of the Lord all the days of my life, to gaze upon the beauty of the Lord and to seek him in his temple" (Psalm 27:4).

Chapter Forty-three

God of Light

(Based on John 3:1-21)

So this is Jesus, I think coolly as I pass a small gathering on my way home from church council. A Man stands in their midst, holding a grimy baby in His arms, talking earnestly with the child's mother.

I kick a pop can from my path. *Good publicity, isn't it?* I think to myself. *Side with the women and you've won half the battle!*

"If you become like a little child," He tells the nodding mother, "you too can enter My kingdom. Children know the secret of salvation."

Jesus, Jesus! I rebuke, nearly tripping over the toes of my shiny new dress shoes in surprise. *You even stoop to bribing the love of the children.* I hurry by the parking lot revival, blocking my ears to another word of His sentimental nonsense.

"Nick, you're being far too hard on Him," Naomi insists when I tell her the story. "Jesus is only a Man, and men make mistakes." She pats my cheek and crosses the kitchen. "Even you."

"But Naomi!" I slam my fist onto the counter, and a few dishes shake in their cupboards. "I *know* He's just a Man—only a fool would call Him God. But I just can't stand His campaigning methods."

"Campaigning methods?" She arches her perfectly formed eyebrows. "What do you mean?"

I snort. "It's obvious that this guy is out to take over the highest position He can attain—by sabotage. He's getting the public to side against us."

"Us?"

"You know, *us.*" I gesture around our spacious home. "The backbone of the church. The pastors who make things happen."

Naomi walks around the counter and begins unloading a bag of groceries. "I don't know about that," she muses under her breath.

"What?"

"If you pastors make so much happen, why did a little boy beg to carry my groceries for only a quarter? He was hungry, Nick. And what have you done to help him?" Her snapping brown eyes demand a reply.

"Who do you think I am? God?" I spread my hands in a helpless gesture. "I can't do it all, Naomi!"

"Exactly." She sighs and picks at a cellophane wrapper. "Nick, when that boy begged to carry my bag today, Jesus walked up with a sandwich. I know He had bought it for Himself, but He tapped that kid on the shoulder and offered it to him anyway." Her eyes shine with unshed tears. "You should have seen the look on that kid's face."

I stalk from the room. "I'm glad I didn't," I hurl over my shoulder at her. "It was probably staged."

"Nick!"

I don't reply. *Jesus,* I mutter at my reflection in the mirror, *You're tearing my family to pieces! Why can't You just leave?* As I take off my elegant tie, I know why Jesus bothers me so much. *He's not with the program.* Gazing around my solid-oak bedroom, I admit that "the program" includes leather Bibles, conference promotions, and hefty church memberships. "And a little respect for tradition." I mutter.

For years it's been the unspoken rule of our church council to massage our members' consciences—and their pocketbooks. Of course we preach the honest gospel, but who needs to cry at every service? Then this Jesus comes along and sabotages our entire plan.

"What's that, Dad?" Mark strides into the room. "Talking to yourself again?"

"What do you need, son?"

He shuffles his feet on the shag-carpeted floor and plays with his newest earring. I bite back a reproving comment. "Well," Mark finally begins. "I was wondering if we could have a father-son discussion. Is that all right?" His left eyebrow twitches, a nervous tic he inherited from me.

"Sure, buddy!" I slap him on the back. "What's on your mind?" *Please,* I think to myself, *don't let this be bad.*

"Dad, your left eyebrow is kind of twitching," Mark laughs as he flops onto my bed.

"Thanks."

"So Christy and I were talking today," he begins. "And we passed by this big K-mart parking lot."

"Yeah?" I cock an eyebrow and try to act calm. "What happened?"

"Well, there was this huge crowd of people gathered around the cart corral, and we thought we might see a fight."

"Haven't I told you to—"

"I know, I know." He holds up a hand. "Just wait."

I shut my mouth obediently.

"Well, we got there and this really tall Man welcomed us in! His name was Jesus—you know, the guy who's been on the radio lately. And He said He was expecting us. Did you tell Him we were coming?"

"No. No, I didn't." My heart falls. *Jesus again?*

"Well, anyway," Mark rushes on, "Jesus is incredible! He's not an ordinary preacher, Dad. He's *interesting!* And Dad, He actually makes me think. Even Christy noticed it."

"That's great, son. Street people fascinate me too."

"But He's not just a street person!" Mark protests. "He's Someone special. And, well, Dad, I was wondering, do you think I could be a preacher like Jesus?"

I open my mouth and close it again. The ticking of our grandfather clock suddenly becomes deafening. Mark watches me carefully, all the hope of new discovery written in his eyes.

"I, uh, well, Mark, I'm behind you all the way," I finally stutter.

"Thanks, Dad!" He jumps to his feet and shakes my hand impulsively. "I gotta run now. Promised Christy we'd watch a movie at her house tonight."

"'Bye, Mark." I stare at his retreating back until he disappears through the garage door. *A preacher like Jesus?* I wonder. *What about becoming a preacher like Dad? What's so wrong about that?*

Suddenly I know what I must do.

Outside, the sun has lowered itself into the heart of the city, and shadows play across the street. *It's now or never. Forget the public image, Nick. He's messing with your family!*

Still wearing my dark business suit, I slip out through the back door. "Be back in a few, honey," I call toward the kitchen. Naomi doesn't answer, and I hope she's running the blender. *She'll never even miss me.*

Carefully I retrace my steps to the rundown K mart where I first saw Him. Every time a car passes I slide behind the nearest telephone pole and scan the vehicle's occupants. *No church councilers in that one,* I sigh in relief.

Then I spot Him rearranging the carts next to K mart Garden Center, and my assurance flees. *Why am I here? The council could blackmail me forever if they find out!*

"Hello." He smiles and pushes a cart into the corral. "I've been waiting for you."

"Right." I suddenly realize that I forgot my tie. "We, uh, we—we"—I fumble with my collar, trying to sound professionally calm—"We've been watching You, Mr. —"

"Just call me Jesus."

I feel like I'm on a mission for the KGB. "Well, Jesus, we've been watching You, and we've decided that Your, ah, *ministry* is very unique. You must be very close to God." I clear my throat and scan the empty lot. If Elder Jones sees me here, my career will be ruined. But I must find out what my family sees in this small-town fanatic that has changed them so radically.

"Why, thank you!" He smiles broadly. "I am rather close to my Father. But as I'm sure you know, no one can live with Him forever unless they're born again."

I gulp and take the plunge. In a cat-and-mouse game of leading questions, I try to find the crack in His facade. But after several minutes I still haven't found a flaw. Jesus seems so relaxed that I wonder if He's arranged for all my church council superiors to stake out the area with video cameras and document my folly.

"I really should be going," I interrupt, edging away from the yellow circle of light we stand in. "It's late, and I'm sure You're very tired—"

"Nick, listen to Me." Jesus holds my gaze, and I can't move another step. "God loves you. He loves you so much that He sent His only Son—Me—down here to die for your sins . . . and Naomi's sins . . . and the sins of Mark and Emma and Christy and all your church council enemies." His words penetrate my resolve to be distant.

"But don't worry, Nick," He continues warmly. "I'm not here to judge you. I'm here to find and rescue every single lost person. And if you believe in Me, you'll never be condemned to die for your sins. I'll take care of them."

"Now Jesus," I interrupt hastily, "You don't understand. I'm a member of—"

"Listen, Nick." He looks deep into my eyes, and I fall silent. "Just listen for a minute." Jesus gestures around the light-dotted parking lot. "Nick, My presence brings the light of truth into this world. But you humans love sin more than truth, so you flee from My light. You're living in the dark! If you really loved the truth, you'd be proud to share your faith with the world without any shame. Don't you agree?"

I cannot respond.

In five minutes Jesus has given me enough food for thought to last a lifetime. I know I should remind Him that I *don't* have faith in Him—yet. But I can't bear to break the silence. Instead, I shuffle slowly from His presence, leaving Him standing in that yellow oasis of light beside a red-handled shopping cart.

I'll probably never see Him again.

You're living in the dark! Jesus' words are still resonating in my mind when I enter my own light-flooded house. *Am I afraid to share my faith?* I wonder silently as I pass our big family Bible, untouched since Christmas Day. *Can I even share it with the ones I love the most?*

"And God, please be with all the missionaries and with Mark and Daddy and my new kitty, Roger." Emma's 4-year-old lisp floats from her bedroom. Naomi kneels with her, her eyes closed in reverent silence. She doesn't even hear me pass the door.

No. My conscience speaks boldly now. *No, I can't even share with my family. And Naomi's prayers with Emma prove it.* I sink into my padded desk chair and stare out our bedroom window. *I don't know who this Jesus is, but He's definitely no pretender.* My reflection stares icily back at me. *Unlike some people I know.*

I analyze my own soft hands and mentally compare them to Jesus' rough callused ones. *Share my faith with the world? Without being ashamed? Where should I begin?*

"Nick, you're back!" Naomi's form fills the bedroom door. "Is everything all right? It's so dark in here!"

Before I can even nod, she walks inside and flips on the light. I'm flooded in a wash of brightness that makes everything glow from within for an instant. I lean back in my chair, and she slides onto my lap. "Naomi," I begin tentatively. "Naomi, what would you think if I started having family worship again?"

I'm out of the dark.

Reference Points:

"The Lord is my light and my salvation—whom shall I fear? The Lord is the stronghold of my life—of whom shall I be afraid?" (Psalm 27:1).

"You are the light of the world. A city on a hill cannot be hidden. Neither do people light a lamp and put it under a bowl. Instead they put it on its stand, and it gives light to everyone in the house. In the same way, let your light shine before men, that they may see your good deeds and praise your Father in heaven" (Matthew 5:14-16).

"This is the message we have heard from him and declare to you: God is light; in him there is no darkness at all. If we claim to have fellowship with him yet walk in the darkness, we lie and do not live by the truth. But if we walk in the light, as he is in the light, we have fellowship with one another, and the blood of Jesus, his Son, purifies us from all sin" (1 John 1:5-7).

Chapter Forty-four

God Who Is

"Karen Coleman, you have a visitor in the lobby. Karen Coleman, you have a visitor in the lobby." The loudspeaker on Senior Hall blares my mother's name. She jumps in surprise and a wide grin spreads across her face.

"That must be my boyfriend!" she calls, throwing on her jacket as she runs toward the stairwell.

Jen, Joie, Caroline, and I watch her departure in amusement.

"Your mom is amazing!" Jen laughs as the stairwell door slams shut behind Mom. "She acts just like I do when someone pages me."

I smile and flop onto my saggy dorm bed. "I'm used to it. My parents are still in the 'teenage' stage of their relationship."

When I mention our conversation later, Mom demands, "And what's wrong with that? Dad and I are just as in love as we were 20 years ago. Why can't we act like it?" She is perched on Dad's lap in their favorite rocking chair.

"No, no," I hastily add. "It doesn't bother me at all. You're an unusual married couple, but I like it."

"So do we." Dad smiles contentedly.

As long as I can remember, my parents' relationship has been a standard that I someday hope to achieve.

Although they've had their share of difficulties, they always survive them together.

"Even though your father and I don't always agree," Mom told me one time, "I think it's important that I support his dreams and goals anyway. We have to work together."

I can't imagine a better arrangement, one in which both parties give 100 percent to make the relationship succeed. My friends often have a rough time because one or both parties doesn't give as much as the other.

"I'll do anything to make this relationship work," someone told me recently. "But I know that Monica just doesn't love me as much as I love her. We could never survive a marriage."

"I've waited for LeAnn for so long," someone else confessed, "but she doesn't seem to care. She's cheated on me, dumped me, forgotten about me, and lied to me. How can I ever trust her again?"

"I like him well enough, but he's just afraid of commitment. We'll never grow unless he's willing to take that risk" seems to be the standard comment of girls.

It's depressing to watch most relationships end in anger or hurt feelings. Usually one person feels mistreated or angry because of the other person's actions. And seldom do former boyfriends/girlfriends ever become "just friends" again.

Sadie and Craig, however, have shattered the dating trend. Several summers ago I spent some time with them while I worked on my writing. Since I was in the middle of a dating crisis of my own, I often asked their opinions on romance-related subjects.

"What makes your relationship so special?" I wondered one afternoon as we sat in Craig's pickup and basked in the air-conditioning it provided.

"Trust," Craig responded immediately. "I trust Sadie completely."

Sadie nodded, then offered her own opinion. "For me it's compatibility. I've gotten to the point where I feel more comfortable with Craig than without him. Somehow he feels like a part of my heart that I never want to lose."

I was awed by their incredible friendship. And a year later, in a movie, I found the perfect phrase to describe what they feel: *You complete me.* I saw a deaf man say it to his girlfriend in sign language. Although I couldn't hear the words, the message stayed so sharply in focus that I remember it still.

You complete me. That's the kind of love I want to find. And believe it or not, that's the kind of love I'm starting to discover. You see, I'm getting to know a wonderful Person. He's caring and sensitive, and He promises to fill my every pore with His love. He says I won't have room for feeling unfulfilled. I won't stay discouraged for long. I'll have a secure hope for the future. I can't be entirely lonely. And I'll certainly never despise my life again.

I know—it sounds too good to be true. But this Person is different. Somehow I know I can trust Him. He's never let me down. In fact He's given His entire life to proving that He cares. And I'd like to do the same for Him.

I'm sure this seems rather sudden. Although I hardly know this Person, I know Him well enough to realize that He, of all the options I have considered, is the only One who can complete my existence. He is "the Alpha and the Omega, the First and the Last, the Beginning and the End" (Revelation 22:13). He is everything I have ever needed or hoped for. He is God, the God I want to spend eternity with, the God who is.

Reference Points:

"Many waters cannot quench love; rivers cannot wash it away. If one were to give all the wealth of his house for love, it would be utterly scorned" (Song of Solomon 8:7).

"My heart says of you, 'Seek his face!' Your face, Lord, I will seek" (Psalm 27:8).

"O Lord, you have searched me and you know me. You know when I sit and when I rise; you perceive my thoughts from afar. You discern my going out and my lying down; you are familiar with all my ways. Before a word is on my tongue you know it completely, O Lord. You hem me in—behind and before; you have laid your hand upon me. Such knowledge is too wonderful for me, too lofty for me to attain. Where can I go from your Spirit? Where can I flee from your presence? If I go up to the heavens, you are there; if I make my bed in

the depths, you are there. If I rise on the wings of the dawn, if I settle on the far side of the sea, even there your hand will guide me, your right hand will hold me fast. If I say, 'Surely the darkness will hide me and the light become night around me,' even the darkness will not be dark to you; the night will shine like the day, for darkness is as light to you. For you created my inmost being; you knit me together in my mother's womb. I praise you because I am fearfully and wonderfully made; your works are wonderful, I know that full well. My frame was not hidden from you when I was made in the secret place. When I was woven together in the depths of the earth, your eyes saw my unformed body. All the days ordained for me were written in your book before one of them came to be. How precious to me are your thoughts, O God! How vast is the sum of them! Were I to count them, they would outnumber the grains of sand. When I awake, I am still with you" (Psalm 139:1-18).

"Can a mother forget the baby at her breast and have no compassion on the child she has borne? Though she may forget, I will not forget you! See, I have engraved you on the palms of my hands; your walls are ever before me" (Isaiah 49:15, 16).